City of London Libraries

Please return on or before the latest date above.

To renew log on to your account at

https://col.ent.sirsidynix.net.uk

or telephone 020 7638 0569 during library opening hours

www.cityoflondon.gov.uk/libraries

Online resources to accompany this book are available at
https://bloomsbury.pub/theory-for-theatre-studies-bodies. If
you experience any problems, please contact Bloomsbury at
companionwebsites@bloomsbury.com.

Theory for Theatre Studies meets the need for accessible, mid-length volumes that unpack keywords that lie at the core of the discipline. Aimed primarily at undergraduate students and secondarily at postgraduates and researchers, the volumes feature both background material historicizing the term and original, forward-looking research into intersecting theoretical trends in the field. Case studies ground volumes in praxis, and additional resources online ensure readers are equipped with the necessary skills and understanding as they move deeper into the discipline.

SERIES EDITORS

Susan Bennett, University of Calgary, Canada
Kim Solga, Western University, Canada

Published titles
Theory for Theatre Studies: Space
Kim Solga
Theory for Theatre Studies: Sound
Susan Bennett
Theory for Theatre Studies: Memory
Milija Gluhovic
Theory for Theatre Studies: Emotion
Peta Tait
Theory for Theatre Studies: Movement
Rachel Fensham

Forthcoming titles
Theory for Theatre Studies: Economics
Michael McKinnie
Theory for Theatre Studies: Aesthetics
John Lutterbie

Theory for Theatre Studies: Bodies

Soyica Diggs Colbert

Series editors: Susan Bennett and Kim Solga

methuen | drama

LONDON · NEW YORK · OXFORD · NEW DELHI · SYDNEY

METHUEN DRAMA
Bloomsbury Publishing Plc
50 Bedford Square, London, WC1B 3DP, UK
1385 Broadway, New York, NY 10018, USA
29 Earlsfort Terrace, Dublin 2, Ireland

BLOOMSBURY, METHUEN DRAMA and the Methuen Drama logo
are trademarks of Bloomsbury Publishing Plc

First published in Great Britain 2022

Series design by Louise Dugdale
Cover image: Origami walking man (© Henrik Sorensen / Getty Images)

A catalogue record for this book is available from the British Library.

A catalog record for this book is available from the Library of Congress.

ISBN: HB: 978-1-4742-4632-3
          PB: 978-1-4742-4631-6
          ePDF: 978-1-4742-4634-7
          eBook: 978-1-4742-4633-0

Series: Theory for Theatre Studies

Typeset by Integra Software Services Pvt. Ltd.
Printed and bound in Great Britain

To find out more about our authors and books visit www.bloomsbury.com
and sign up for our newsletters.

For Rodger

CONTENTS

SECTION THREE

SERIES PREFACE

Theory for Theatre Studies (TfTS) is a series of introductory theoretical monographs intended for both undergraduate and postgraduate students as well as researchers branching out into fresh fields. It aims to introduce constellations of ideas, methods, theories, and rubrics central to the working concerns of scholars in theater and performance studies at the opening of the twenty-first century. With a primary focus on twentieth-century developments, TfTS volumes offer accessible and provocative engagements with critical theory that inspire new ways of thinking theory in important disciplinary and interdisciplinary modes.

The series features full-length volumes explicitly aimed at unpacking sets of ideas that have coalesced around carefully chosen key terms in theater and performance, such as space, sound, bodies, memory, movement, economies, and emotion. TfTS volumes do not aggregate existing essays, but rather provide a careful, fresh synthesis of what extensive reading by our authors reveals to be key nodes of interconnection between among theoretical models. The goal of these texts is to introduce readers to a wide variety of critical approaches and to unpack the complex theory useful for both performance analysis and creation.

Each volume in the series focuses on one specific set of theoretical concerns, constellated around a term that has become central to understanding the social and political labor of theater and performance work at the turn of the millennium. The organization of each book follows a common template: Section 1 includes a historical overview of interconnected theoretical models, Section 2 features extended case studies using twentieth- and twenty-first-century performances, and

Section 3 looks ahead, as our authors explore important new developments in their constellation. Each volume is broad enough in scope to look laterally across its topic for compelling connections to related concerns, yet specific enough to be comprehensive in its assessment of its particular term. The ideas explored and explained through lively and detailed case studies provide diverse critical approaches for reading all kinds of plays and performances as well as starting points for practical exploration.

Each book includes a Further Reading section and features a companion website with chapter summaries, questions for discussion, and a host of video and other web links.

Susan Bennett (University of Calgary, Canada)
and Kim Solga (Western University, Canada)

ACKNOWLEDGMENTS

In some ways, every book extends an ongoing line of thought. This book builds on work I began in my first book, *The African American Theatrical Body* and, therefore, I am indebted to all of the individuals and institutions that have contributed to the development of my thought from then until now. It is a list that is too extensive to name, but I would like to take the opportunity to honor the indelible imprint that Cheryl A. Wall has left on my work. Without her guidance, example, and care, none of my work would exist. I am grateful to have had her as a mentor and friend and hope my work reflects positively on her legacy.

In addition, thank you to the Georgetown University Idol Family Professorship endowment fund and the Georgetown University Healey Family Endowed Fund for Academic Excellence for their financial support, which enabled research assistance essential to completing this project. The generosity of the series editors, Susan Bennett and Kim Solga, has enriched this book; I am grateful for their support.

Finally, I must thank my family. I've learned over the years that writing a book has a deep impact on all of those closest to you. Thank you to the Brown Family, R. Harrington Diggs, Joanne Diggs, Diallyo Diggs, Rakiya Moore, and Diallyo Diggs II. And to Rodger Colbert, you gather me and make me better. Thank you!

Bodies: An Introduction

The Royal Shakespeare Company's 2016 production of *Hamlet* opens with the titular figure, played by Ghanaian-British actor Paapa Essiedu, graduating from college. In the first moments of the performance recording, taped live in Stratford-upon-Avon, music plays, school bells ring, and a school official wearing commencement attire and standing before an audience calls "Hamlet, Prince of Denmark." Essiedu walks through the audience, up the stairs, onto the stage, and toward the school official, hugging fellow graduates along the way. Essiedu as Hamlet is handed his diploma and looks off into the distance to pose for a picture with the official. The snapping sound of a camera shutter and flash of the bulb frames the moment and Essiedu as Hamlet. The opening scene establishes the particular ways he will appear as the titular figure in the production: young, Black, and male. Essiedu the actor specifies the character of Hamlet through his physical appearance, the history it draws forth, and the contexts established in the 2016 production of the play. As performance studies theorist Judith Butler teaches, the audience ascribes meaning to Blackness, maleness, and youth before entering the theater. Essiedu may affirm or challenge the audience's expectations for his race, gender, and age but his identity emerges as an exchange between his physical presentation and the audience members' varied perceptions. Together the structuring of the opening scene and the audience's expectations of identity categories (race, gender, and age) script the appearance of Essiedu as Hamlet. While drama depends on the suspension of disbelief and assumes that actors use their bodies to represent other characters, if an actor or role is well known, the shift from actor to character requires greater care.

In the opening paragraph, I described Essiedu playing Hamlet to call attention to how the play established him as the figure on stage. In this case, the production created an opening sequence to facilitate identifying the prince. It is my contention that this opening sequence works to establish Essiedu as Hamlet against the backdrop of other actors playing the role and the presumption that Hamlet is white. In so doing, Essiedu and the production team draw from the experiences that endow his young, Black, male body with meaning, both personal and historical.

As a performing art, theater foregrounds physical bodies in motion. Casting Essiedu as Hamlet calls attention to not only the history of his body as a young (born 1990), Black person but also the history of bodies that have embodied the role of Hamlet. Through movement, presentation, narration, costuming, and interaction with theatrical devices, actors' bodies come to embody a role. In addition, the actor must draw from the experiences that give meaning to his or her body. Essiedu's body has meaning in the world because of the histories, material and discursive, associated with Blackness, maleness, and age. The meaning created through an actor's body on stage always draws from multiple histories: the history of the embodiment of the role, the history of experiences that give the actor's body meaning for the actor and the audience. *Theory for Theatre Studies: Bodies* explores how the ideas of theorists from Karl Marx to Michel Foucault to Judith Butler apply in the context of an art form that has theorized the body for centuries, endowing it with meaning while contending with the way it carries meaning forth into every theatrical event. Marx explores how labor and economic conditions shape the body. Foucault examines how power structures inform perceptions of the body. And Butler considers how desire, discursive practices, and the repetition of behavior produce the body. All three theorists understand the body as emerging in relationship to discursive, historical, and material networks that set expectations for individuals before they step on the scene or on the stage.

In response to how race shaped his preparation for the part of Hamlet, Essiedu responds, "A lot of people ask, 'What does it feel like to be a black man playing Hamlet?' That's a stupid question. It's not like I woke up one day and remembered I was black. It's part of my everyday experience" (Wise 2018). Instead of considering how Essiedu forms himself to play the role, his response suggests that the role must apply to him as the actor with a wealth of experiences from which to draw, including how one comports the racialized body and shapes it to play a role. The setting of the production in Africa makes Essiedu's heritage a useful point of reference, but he is clear that as an actor he does not constantly translate his Blackness but rather draws from it as a part of his professional identity.

Judith Butler's *Gender Trouble* (1990) and *Bodies That Matter* (1995) produced a foundational change in thinking for scholars in Theatre and Performance Studies by theorizing the construction of gender and the mutability of the body. Butler's work built on a long history of scholarship, including in the nineteenth century Friedrich Nietzsche's *Genealogy of Morals*, in the mid-twentieth century existentialists such as Simone de Beauvoir, Richard Wright, Lorraine Hansberry, and Jean-Paul Sartre, and in the late-twentieth-century women of color feminists—among them, Gloria Anzaldúa, Ntozake Shange, and Audre Lorde—that considered how discursive histories, power structures, and practices shape the body. An outgrowth of a long history of theorizing the body, Butler's writing crystalized a set of ideas about how language and physical movement endow the body with meaning that both precedes its emergence on stage and frames it once it arrives. Social conventions produce anticipation of a white actor playing Hamlet and how, as an audience member, we meet Essiedu in the role. Does seeing him as Hamlet produce excitement, disappointment, curiosity, confusion, frustration, or some mix therein? What attachments do audiences bring to the theater and project onto the bodies of actors?

Butler calls attention to the strong pull that history and social convention have on the materialization of gender in particular. Her work ushered in a reconsideration of gender as fixed and then, subsequently although not easily, endowed individuals with greater agency. In the preface to the 1999 edition of *Gender Trouble*, Butler reflects:

> The anticipation of an authoritative disclosure of meaning is the means by which that authority is attributed and installed: the anticipation conjures its object. I wondered whether we do not labor under a similar expectation concerning gender, that it operates as an interior essence that might be disclosed, an expectation that ends up producing the very phenomenon that it anticipates. In the first instance, then, the performativity of gender revolves around the metalepsis, the way in which the anticipation of a gendered essence produces that which it posits as outside itself. Secondly, performativity is not a singular act, but a repetition and a ritual, which achieves its effects through its naturalization in the context of a body, understood, in part, as a culturally sustained temporal duration. (1999: xiv–xv)

Drawing and departing from existentialist thought that asserts "Existence precedes essence; or, if you prefer, that subjectivity must be our point of departure," Butler explains how the individual discovers gender in relationship to the anticipation of others (Sartre 2007: 20). In his essay "Existentialism is a Humanism," originally published in 1947, Sartre does not focus or concede the formation of subjectivity as intersubjective but does establish that existence precedes the individual's subjectivity. Similar to de Beauvoir, Butler adds the understanding of subjectivity as a class.

Butler distinguishes "gender" as a part of an individual's subjectivity from "the performativity of gender" as a social construct that has a history attached to communal desires. She emphasizes the difficulty of transforming the social scripts that make normative forms of gender presentation legible. Such transformation would require interrupting the flow of ideas, associations, or assumption, a "metalepsis"—a narrative intrusion—in which gender performativity lays claim on an individual's gender. Analogizing Butler's analysis of gender roles to theatrical ones, the excitement and anticipation of Hamlet's physical appearance call forth casting choices and expectations for the role. The 2016 production of *Hamlet* participates in what Butler describes as metalepsis—the shift of a figure in a text from one position to another, drawing attention to the constructed nature of the text. By calling Essiedu to the role of Hamlet through the graduation scene, the 2016 production breaks the illusion that the actor is the character but also, in this case, creates room for Essiedu to be Hamlet. Butler's interventions in understandings of gender and the materialization of the body emphasize humans' unique ability to change. Her work, however, does not require such an understanding of human beings as singular and separate from the social, environmental, and political contexts in which they act.

The opening of the Royal Shakespeare Company's 2016 production of *Hamlet* introduces the audience to the actors playing the roles and sets the foundation for the actors to establish themselves as the characters. In a familiar role like Hamlet, an actor must convince an audience that he is the Prince of Denmark, assuming that viewers have previously seen others enact the role. Essiedu is the first Black actor to play Hamlet in the history of the Royal Shakespeare Company. As a result, he was repeatedly asked to reflect on his preparation for the historic production and the significance of his being cast in the role. In rehearsals, Essiedu explains, "An actor has to understand what they are saying, and so does the actor they are talking to. If that happens, then the audience will understand, too. So, when we're rehearsing we spend a huge amount of time paraphrasing what Shakespeare is saying so we're all clear on the meaning" (Lovell 2018). Essiedu explains that to play the role he first had to translate the action of the play to familiar words and scenarios.

The shaping of the production helps to establish Essiedu in the role but so too do his personal experiences. As Louis Wise reports in the *Sunday Times*, "Essiedu brought two distinct things to the table: first, his deeply felt African heritage, both his parents being Ghanaian; and second, his experience of grief, both those parents having passed away. His father, who lived in Ghana, died when he was 14; his mother, who brought him up in a single-parent home, when he was 20" (Wise 2018). Essiedu explains, "For me, grief was an obsessive focus when I was taking the part" (Wise 2018). In considering how to animate the character, how to shape the character's physical movements in the play, Essiedu drew from his own experience of mourning the loss of his parents. Considering the loss of a parent as a life-altering event that most people experience, Essiedu particularizes the impact for a young person not just on how one processes information but also on behaviors and interactions. For example, early in the play he cries out and crouches in anguish at the realization that his mother and uncle have married and they want him to remain home and discontinue his studies abroad. He continues, "A lot of people look at the play and think, 'Oh, I don't get why he treats so-and-so like that—what is that madness thing about?' They're trying to apply the logic of somebody who's totally fine. But we're talking about somebody who has suffered incredible trauma" (Wise 2018). The experience of grief has a physical manifestation in the body that Essiedu draws from to communicate Hamlet's loss.

In addition to the specificity of Essiedu's age as a characteristic of how his body will appear to a viewer, the audience most certainly marks the racial difference of the cast, if the repeated questions from reporters serve as evidence of audience responses to the production. Although in the comments cited above, Essiedu does not make reference to the changes the 2016 production makes to the setting of the play, the action takes place in an African kingdom that draws influence from West African and Caribbean cultures. When Hamlet and the other characters appear on stage, the setting helps establish what will make this version of *Hamlet* distinct. The costumes also introduce the audience to a modern Hamlet that lives in a world infused with references from the global Black diaspora, including clothing and music. How does clothing, from the suit that Hamlet wears to the African robes donned by his mother and uncle to the uniforms of the guards, indicate the specific role characters play in society and how the audience should interpret their physical presentation? How do costumes prescribe audiences' perceptions of the actors and their bodies?

In the opening moments of the play, Essiedu has the added pressure of not only the general charge to appear as his character, but also to do so is perhaps one of the most well-known roles in Western drama. His performance then expands the role and invites audiences to reconsider what they know about the character and the history of Hamlet's characterization as older and white. Quoting playwright Lorraine Hansberry, Harry J. Elam, Jr. explains, "Theater is built upon devices. In the theatrical environment, the signification of objects results from their specific usage in the moment … Every theatrical performance depends on performers' and spectators' collaborative consciousness of the devices in operation and their meanings. This consciousness is coconstructed in a new way with each performance" (2001: 5). Essiedu's race and age, his physical appearance, and his body serve as devices deployed in the play to expand the meaning of *Hamlet*, Hamlet, and Blackness on stage.

The physical body figures so strongly that theater features dead, resurrected, and ghostly figures, yet still embodied. While death marks the demise of the physical body, theater's presentation of ghostly figures draws attention to the body as an idea and an ideal, something we attach with meaning, desire, and aspirations. In the 2016 production, the ghost of Hamlet's dead father is "played majestically by Ewart James Walters, wrapped in Kente (traditional Ghanaian) cloth" (Treneman 2016). He "is the elder who must be obeyed. In

Africa, Essiedu has said, spirits are seen as a much more tangible part of life and here the ghost is still, commanding and imperious" (Treneman 2016). In the play, African drumming precedes Hamlet's encountering his father's ghost. Suggesting the apparition possesses Hamlet, the titular character writhes on the floor in advance of the appearance. The ghost, fully clothed and commanding, sets Hamlet on his mission of vengeance that will animate the remainder of the play.

The physical presentation of ghostly figures draws attention to how the materialization of the body—the ways the body comes to have meaning and hold space, value, and weight in the world—works between the limit points of life and death. Theater requires using material devices, including the body, to communicate symbolic, psychological, and metaphorical ideas. As a result, the body often serves as a screen that does not call attention to its mutability (see Cheng 2013). In the case of presenting figures that have transcended death, however, such as the dead ancestors of the central character Prior Walter in *Angels in America*, Part 2, that I discuss in Section 2, theater calls attention to bodies as animated by ideas about not only life and death but also about living and dying. How do belief systems, social, cultural, and economic conditions, and communal and familial contexts inform our understandings and experiences of the body?

The body's centrality to dramatic action may seem self-evident, or, at least, the truth of what the body represents may seem to be given unless a play itself calls the body's presentation into question. Given that theater produces its own theories of the body, this book offers a historical overview of how theater theorizes the body alongside an engagement with modern theorists whose work expands understandings of the body in theater studies. In the first section of this book, I explore theatrical conventions from the medieval period to the present that inform how bodies appear on stage. How do theatrical conventions participate in, question, and complicate contemporary theories of the body? In the medieval, early modern, and Enlightenment periods, theater relied on the seeming verisimilitude—the appearance of truth or reality—of the body, but by the nineteenth century, artists and scholars began to reconsider the presentation of the body as self-evident. While the body has long been staged and animated in theaters to call forth complex histories and participate in citational practices and belief systems, in modernity artists and scholars routinely embed questions about the presentation of bodies on stage: How do we know the race, gender, or sex of this character? Is the character living or dead and what distinguishes the two states? Who decides the meaning of the character's physical characteristics—the performers, the playwright, or the audience?

In the late twentieth century, theater asked questions about whether or not one can arrive at a unified truth of the body (how do the audience and the actor know the race, gender, or sex of a character?). Although, in the late twentieth century, theorists arrived at a clear articulation of how history, power, position, and psychic attachments form understandings of the body, theater performances from medieval drama to the contemporary period have wrangled with the meaning of the body in relationship to the soul and the mind, as a manifestation of power, and a result of culture. Theatrical conventions engage with, expand upon, and articulate theories of the body, furthering and defining social, religious, and cultural understandings. For example, Section 1 considers how medieval drama engaged Christian beliefs about the body's relationship to the soul. What are the implications of medieval drama's conventions for representation of the body to a historical and theoretical understanding of the body? Throughout Section 1, I explore what new theatrical conventions are developed in the medieval, early modern, and Enlightenment periods to produce theories of the body. How do shifts in understanding of agency inform theories of the body for actors as well as audiences?

The theatrical conventions that govern interactions on and off stage also inform how the body appears within a given historical period. In the nineteenth century, as I also explore in Section 1, theater practices began to actively challenge conventions governing the appearance of bodies rather than assuming or confirming them. Artists, scholars, politicians, and activists began to question the strict distinction between races. Dion Boucicault's *The Octoroon* (1852) presents a classic story of the tragic mixed race figure that appears white but must suffer due to her mixed-race lineage. The play hinges on the sympathy an audience feels for a figure that appears white but "is" Black. Similar to the Supreme Court case *Plessy V. Ferguson* (1896) that affirms the legality of segregation in the United States, *The Octoroon* questions if racial designation is a physical or biological marker. Legal theories of the body often became fodder for theatrical theories in the nineteenth century (see Brooks 2006). To comedic effect, Lynn Nottage's *By the Way, Meet Vera Stark* (2011) explores similar questions about the relationship between race and physical appearance, presenting a phenotypically white mixed race figure but in the context of 1930s Hollywood. In Nottage's play, the central character, Vera Stark, never achieves the fame of her white presenting cousin, Gloria Mitchell. The mixed-race figure, Gloria, in Nottage's play does not have a tragic ending like the one in *The Octoroon* but rather emblematizes the privilege and ongoing instability of whiteness in the twentieth century. While nineteenth-century American legal precedent confirmed race as a biological category, theater practices have troubled clear-cut racial biological distinctions. Theater negotiates different sources of knowledge about economic and cultural systems rather than the body alone.

While late-twentieth- and early-twenty-first-century theater productions and critical theories both explore how we ascribe meaning to physical differences, the presence of the body on stage also draws attention to training practices that account for contemporary political and social debates. In 2017, sexual-abuse allegations against film producer Harvey Weinstein elevated the use of Tarana Burke's hashtag #MeToo, which had first circulated in 2006 to draw attention to the pervasiveness of sexual harassment and assault. Also in 2006, Tonia Sina, creator of the Intimacy for the Stage method and co-founder and executive director of Intimacy Directors International, first used the term "intimacy choreography" to draw attention to the necessity of staging scenes of intimacy just as directors call in experts to stage fight scenes (Purcell 2018). Similar to fight choreography, intimacy choreography acknowledges the potential for physical injury in depicting sexual encounters on stage and the need for technical direction to protect the actors: "An intimacy director or coordinator encourages the navigation of a scene, through the negotiation of an actor's boundaries of physical touch. It's nuanced choreography, but it also facilitates a conversation between the production and the actors that affirms trust in what's taking place" (Badham 2018). Although intimacy choreographers have been working to support actors since the early 2000s, there has been more widespread attention to the necessity of their expertise since the Weinstein allegations and conviction.

The risk associated with live theater emerges from the impulse to use versions of the Stanislavski system, which calls for putting the actor in the place of and drawing from prior experiences to better understand the motivations of characters (as the interviews with Essiedu suggest he used to depict the loss of a parent in *Hamlet*). In terms of sexual intimacy, the inherent power dynamics in relationships may put actors at risk when transposed to an interaction on stage. Drawing from an actor's past may have unintended negative impacts in the case of intimacy choreography because transposing experiences and emotions in this case also requires coming into close physical contact with another person. So, the movement of the actor's body has a direct physical impact on another actor while, at the same time, directors and scene partners don't know the history from which an individual draws reference. As a result, directors have begun to develop protocols that focus on consent and technical direction in order to safely position the actors' bodies. Histories circulating in relationship to the body, whether personal or communal, require great care to navigate as they inform physical action on stage and the ideological impact for the audience. Just as physical bodies have histories that staging calls forth, so do physical interactions. For example, consider the fervor that attended early twenty-first-century African American actor, singer, and activist Paul Robeson playing Othello in 1943 and the anxiety about the depiction of interracial violence not as a historical relic of the Renaissance drama but as a contemporary early twentieth-century possibility. Robeson's ability to play a Moor violating a white woman risked recalling the fear that a Black man could violate a white woman.

Theatrical presentations of the body intervene in contemporary theories about the body and advance understandings of their own, offering both a reflection on current theories and a comment on them as well. "Through theatre, medieval or modern," the body nevertheless serves as a site to "ponder the interplay between truth and lies, authenticity and inauthenticity, fact and fiction, truth and verisimilitude" (Enders 2019: 4). Tracing conventions for bodies in the theater from the Medieval period to the Modern one calls attention to (1) the body's circulation in religious and secular discourse, (2) the relationship between the body, mind, and spirit through Enlightenment philosophy, (3) the body's relationship to understandings of identity through psychoanalytic, Marxist, and semiotic theories, (4) the body as a source of knowledge and not just a reflection of it through post-structuralist theories, and (5) the body as a source of connection to other bodies conceptually (family) and physically (touch) through phenomenological theories.

Section 1

The first section of the book takes up the historical presentation of the body on stage from the Medieval period to the present and examines how the theater affirmed religious understandings of the body and also helped to develop secular beliefs about the body and its meaning. Theater contributed to theories of the body largely through affirmation, but, in the Renaissance period for example, it did offer sly reconsiderations of cultural assumptions including those about gender. Section 1 offers a historical overview of Western theater theories of the body, calling attention to how theatrical presentation intersected with and diverged from predominant views in Western philosophy. While focusing on Western theater and theories, this section (and the larger book) does not center white European notions of the normative body, but rather calls attention to the influence they have had on understanding the body in an anglophone context. The idea of what it means to be human emerged in the West in relationship to religious and secular doctrine, informing theatrical presentation as well as bodily and embodied knowledge.

In the medieval period, the pageant form resembled contemporary Easter and Christmas rituals in that community members celebrated the high holidays in the Christian faith and through reenactments not only remembered the significance of the day but also learned a religious lesson. The ritual presentation of biblical stories sought to discipline the body and educate the community. Interactive learning through pageant performance functions similarly to the ritual of communion in baptism that uses physical action to symbolize and recall religious sacrifice. The symbolic transformation of the body through reenactment sought to change the communal and individual body to a more pious whole. The experience of embodied learning sought to discipline the unruly sinful body and demonstrate the power of the spirit. Fundamental to the practice was the understanding that the body functions in service to the spirit and that transgressions belong primarily to the body. As a result, these theatrical rituals sought to train the body through behavior.

The hierarchy of mind and spirit over the body continues into the early modern (or Renaissance) period and informs not only the way playwrights present the body on stage but also conventions around staging and casting. Emphasis on certain bodies (white and male) having greater access to transcendence comes to the foreground. William Shakespeare's *Othello*, *Taming of the Shrew*, and *The Tempest* offer useful examples of how different bodies operate in Renaissance drama. Hierarchies among bodies, however, did not disrupt the hierarchy of the spirit and mind over the body. Although theater practices could shape the body, it remained fundamentally flawed, unruly, and dangerous.

Importantly, theorization of the body, even within Western contexts, does not fully account for the enslaved or the colonized. Here I turn to comparative analysis to explore how a twentieth-century Afro-Caribbean playwright, Aimé Césaire, engages in conversation with Shakespeare to draw attention to guiding assumptions about the body in the earlier period. I use a method in Section 1 which not only situates modern plays as works of art but also as theoretical ones. This mode of inquiry, calling attention to guiding assumptions and investigating or interrogating them, is called deconstruction; it emerged in the late twentieth century and I explain it more fully later in this Introduction. Shakespeare's *The Tempest* offers a window into the way systems of oppression shape the body but does not fully account for colonial violence. To make the structure of colonialism decipherable to a popular audience, Césaire's *A Tempest* (1969) performs a cultural translation of *The Tempest* that deemphasizes the perspective of the colonizer and foregrounds the irreverent, insurgent, and humorous one of the colonized. Césaire's play turns the world on its head and upsets the given order of things, depicting the physical, psychological, and social effects of the colonial scene Shakespeare depicted.

Césaire's theater serves as an ideal place to expose how colonization impacts the individual's consciousness and therefore how one perceives the physical presentation of characters in a play because it requires the audiences' tacit participation in the production and draws attention to the social component of the colonial subject's alienation. While all audience members may not identify with the position of the character Caliban as a colonial subject, *A Tempest* provides a space in which to see "what s/he can't see: a sign system *as* a sign system" (Diamond 1997: 47). For example, in Césaire's play Prospero calls Caliban an "ugly ape," and Caliban quips, "You think I'm ugly ... well, I don't think you're so handsome yourself. With that big hooked nose, you look just like some old vulture"—the characters trade in racial stereotypes to draw into question the histories that determine beauty (1992: 16). They also call attention to how the physical body historically has been associated with other animals and therefore deemed a lesser source of knowledge.

Taking a syncretic approach, Césaire created a ritual theater. In the prologue, "the actors enter singly, at random, and each chooses for himself a mask at leisure" (1992: 7). Next, the Master of Ceremonies comments on the individual's choices, but makes clear the roles are arbitrary and require improvisation. Césaire's inclusion of masks clarifies the social dynamic at the heart of his theater. The masks disrupt verisimilitude and invite the audience to participate in the play, to identify with the characters and not necessarily the particular individuals playing the characters. Through the use of masks, the play displays how the adorning of the body produces the character and destabilizes a correlation of race and gender with social station. Just as historically Hamlet has appeared white, colonial subjects have appeared Black and brown (a typical casting choice for the actor playing Caliban in late-twentieth-century productions). *A Tempest* calls attention to the historic and therefore mutable nature of these associations. The choice of masks also underscores the colonized and colonizer as positions of power rather than racially pre-determined roles. Considering Césaire's rendering of Shakespeare's play offers a model of reading that decenters whiteness and the ways the body has been formed in Western thought. I continue this comparative analysis in Section 1 through my examination of the medieval drama *Everyman* and Branden Jacobs-Jenkins' *Everybody* (2017) and then Dion Boucicault's nineteenth-century play *The Octoroon* and Jacobs-Jenkins' *An Octoroon* (2014). I ask, what does the appearance of the body teach us about how history, power, culture, religion, and social context materialize the body?

Although, as stated above, the medieval and Renaissance periods open the door to theorize the body as a construction—as something that we know and understand through history, language, power dynamics, physical interaction, and social and communal practices—it is not until the Enlightenment period that theater makers and theorists begin to question the relationship between the mind and body. Rather than assuming the hierarchy of the body over the mind, in the Enlightenment period the body began to be understood as a source of knowledge in a reciprocal relationship with the mind.

Even as understandings of the relationship between the body and mind shifted, underlying premises of theater remained intact. One premise is that bodies may appear to audiences differently than how they are understood onstage and that the relay between actor and audience produces meaning. Therefore, in the Renaissance period, when young men play women characters, the convention suggests that playing the role has some implication for how we understand gender but not how we understand the actors playing the roles. The conventions of theater pre-twentieth century draw a sharp distinction between the make-believe world of theater and the performance of gender in everyday life because in premodern worldviews gender and race represented physical characteristics that predetermined ways of being in the world. The fundamental difference of biology prescribed identity until the late twentieth century.

In the nineteenth century, as the regulation of bodies intensified in the Americas and Europe, the way the body served as a source of knowledge became increasingly complicated. While darker skin was associated with Blackness, playwrights and politicians began to wonder how to account for Black people that appeared to be white, figures with unruly bodies that did not faithfully present their biology. Either in terms of race or gender or their intersection, theater began to explore the drive toward, and limits of, categorizing bodies in the law. Once again, the body spoke back from the stage to the disciplinary regimes that tried to curtail its expression. In the twentieth century, theorists begin to understand the body as a source of knowledge and connection. The process of producing theater not only changes the creators but hopefully the audience as well. Through the process, people not only learn, they do, which in turn shapes how and what we learn.

In *Bodies*, I explore how Western theater has shaped philosophical theories of the body, sometimes reflecting and in other moments challenging current societal belief systems. In this first section, I establish the theatrical conventions that guide theater making from the medieval period to the present. As mentioned above, the case studies pair *Everyman* with *Everybody* and *The Octoroon* with *An Octoroon* to establish how the contemporary works have a discursive relationship with the earlier ones that establishes a theory of the body. The pairing of *Everyman* and *Everybody* calls attention to the shift from religious to secular framings of the body and thus also to a loosening of the understanding of the body as subordinate to the spirit. Even the title of the play shifts emphasis from the universal male figure to all human beings. In the case of *The Octoroon* and *An Octoroon*, I also consider how the pair intercedes in key theoretical debates about the body concerning regimes of power, how the body circulates in culture, and the emergence of the celebrity or distinctive body.

Section 2

While much of contemporary theories of the body reflect shifts in Western thought following the Second World War, they also have a longer history connected to late-nineteenth- and early-twentieth-century theories of totalizing structures for understanding individual behavior—for example, in Marxism and psychoanalysis. In this second section, I consider how, after the Second World War, scholars began to question the emancipatory potential of all-encompassing systems and, at the same time, to ask whether individuals could meaningfully impact these structures. On the one hand, scholars of the Frankfurt school (such as Walter Benjamin, Max Horkheimer, and Theodor Adorno) considered how the pull of competing world systems informed the shape of history and subjectivity. The use of nuclear warfare to end the Second World War produced the capacity for major global powers to destroy themselves and others, which left an indelible mark on thinkers and called attention to the fragility of life. In terms of the body, thinkers began to consider how the materiality of the body linked to disparate material conditions because of competing political, economic, and social systems. As a result, drawing from Marxism—primarily an economic understanding of human and social relationships—theories of the body began to account for how labor and ideology informed perceptions of the body. At the same time, existentialists contemplated the individual's ability, or lack thereof, to intercede in transforming their conditions. The act of transformation, through word and deed, draws attention to the animation of the body and its place in existentialist thought.

Based on some of the foundational work in mid-twentieth-century thought, later scholars (particularly Foucault) began to articulate theories which called attention to power as constantly circulating between people rather than being located with a monarch or other political leader. Their work—defined as post-structuralism—takes on the organization of language, ideas about identity, and the configuration of institutions. Perhaps most importantly, post-structuralism can be associated with the idea that identity is a construction. The easy assertion that identity is a construction does not fully communicate the historical, social, and economic forces that support certain forms of gender, for example, and discourage other ones. It does, however, emphasize the processes necessary to present bodies and institutions as materially fixed and immutable. The work of post-structuralist feminists in the late-twentieth century also called attention to the uneven history of bodily fixity. For example, while some European bodies may have seemed to serve as the material basis for certain theories of subjectivity, Saidiya Hartman's *Scenes of Subjection* (1997) clarified that Black people's bodies gained meaning as a result of their fungibility: the status of the Black body results from white people's ability to define the bodies of the enslaved by projecting meaning, value, thoughts, and desires onto them even in precise opposition to Black peoples' lived reality. Suzan-Lori Parks's *Father Comes Home from the Wars* (Parts 1, 2, and 3), a case study in Section 2, extends Hartman's theorization of the enslaved body to not only consider how the enslaved's fungibility facilitates their bondage but also their freedom.

While Section 1 is organized historically, offering pairings of case studies to elucidate the prevailing theories of the body across time, Section 2 more specifically takes up the movement from theories of structuralism to post-structuralism and deconstruction. Using three case studies—Jean Genet's *The Balcony* (1957), Tony Kushner's *Angles in America: A Gay Fantasia on a National Theme* (Part 1: 1991 and Part 2: 1992), and *Father Comes Home from the Wars* (Parts 1, 2, and 3) (2014)—I elucidate how each play animates theories of the body. Post-structuralism emerges in the late twentieth century as a response to linguist Ferdinand de Saussure's description of language as "a total system [that] is complete at every moment, no matter what happens to have been altered in it a moment before" (cited in Jameson 1972: 6). Saussure proposed that language gains meaning by an internal system (a structure), not through references to things exterior to it. Meaning or truth does not depend on some external "real" material condition or historical influence. Saussure's theories had impact not only on linguistic studies but on cultural production more generally, suggesting that systems of meaning had internal structures separate from and not determined by material conditions.

Post-structuralism questioned this closed encasement of systems and instead argued for circuits of meaning. Advanced most forcefully by French philosophers Jacques Derrida and Foucault, post-structuralists challenge the idea that meaning is fixed and instead argue for multiple ways to experience the truth. Similarly, deconstruction, a method of reading, considers how the reader's engagement with a text may alter the systems inherent to a text. Deconstruction ushers in the idea that cultural production occurs as a relationship between the object or event and the audience or reader. The object does not have an inherent meaning but comes to have meaning through engagement. Returning to the example that opened this introduction, as Elam Jr. explains, the 2016 production of *Hamlet* comes to have meaning through the circuit of exchange between performers and audience. Theater produces meaning through exchange. Not only do the actors bring experiences that give meaning to their bodies and inform how they embody roles, audience members carry histories that inform how they perceive an actor and a role. A play produces meaning by drawing forth a new, shared understanding between performers and audience members.

The idea of embodied action producing our understanding of people, identities, and groups informed the twentieth-century concept of performance. As Diana Taylor explains in "Translating Performance," "Performance functions as vital acts of transfer, transmitting social knowledge, memory, and a sense of identity through reiterated or what Richard Schechner has called 'twice-behaved behavior'" (2007: 381). Schechner also uses the term "restored behavior," to mark "twice-behaved behavior" as "actions that are not-for-the-first time, prepared, or rehearsed. A person may not be aware that she is performing a strip of restored behavior" (2002: 22). Defining performance in terms of history and time, as an acknowledgment that part of how we recognize an action is because we have seen it before and associate it with a certain web of understandings, demonstrates the power transmitted through action as performance. "Performance" accounts for the repetition embedded in action and the power such repetition wields. Some actions become so familiar and recognizable that they crystalize into identities or, as I describe above, what performance studies scholars call "performatives," which Butler theorizes. When we name a gender identity we assert the perception of stasis, even though daily acts must perpetuate to maintain gender. The practice of articulating one's pronouns, for example, disrupts the stasis of gender, calling attention to its enactment. Nevertheless, individuals name their gender upon introduction and then, unless restated, lapse into a sense of fixity; once introduced gender remains seemingly fixed. As Taylor writes, "To say that something is a performance amounts to an ontological affirmation" (2007: 381). While the idea of "performance" disrupts traditional understandings of ontology, of being, the force of that interruption intensifies when a disruption in the accumulative posture of repetition occurs. This is why it is important to consider forms of performance that do not fit neatly into or that challenge western white, European normative assumptions. In these moments, the formative quality of the body's meaning-making capacity comes to the foreground.

Section 2 historicizes the shifts in theory from structuralism to post-structuralism. I consider how Jean Genet's *The Balcony*, Tony Kushner's *Angels in America* and Suzan-Lori Parks's *Father Comes Home from the Wars* (Parts 1, 2, and 3) not only serve as key touchstones in theater history but also reflect historical and political shifts. The theory that theater develops in the late twentieth and early twenty-first centuries helps to illuminate the social and cultural shifts that feed into philosophical developments. In my reading of *The Balcony,* I focus on how the brothel challenges the perceptions of the real in order to decipher the extent and impact of human agency. In the play, a city erupts in violence while the world of a brothel, the setting of the play, continues to function as a house of mirrors, constructing reality seemingly independent of the surrounding destruction.

Scenes toggle back and forth between physical reality and staged reality, drawing attention to a central question in theater and performance studies: How does one distinguish between the real and the fake? I focus on how post-structuralism challenges a Marxist analysis and specifically an understanding of the relationship between embodied actions and effects.

In the second part of Section 2, I examine *Angels in America* and the specific ways understandings of the body shift in the late twentieth century in response to changes in belief systems. The play examines how the diseased body forms new psychoanalytic understandings and how those understandings relate to post-structuralist notions of power. If power circulates and informs perceptions, experiences, depictions, and categorizations of the body, how does illness add another layer to that equation? Additionally, as new understandings of gender and sexuality emerge in the period, how do presumptions about psychic attachments, kinship, and social roles shift? How are those roles informed by understandings of what relationships engender care and which ones require being cared for? What are our responsibilities to one another and how do those responsibilities get blurred in periods of crisis?

The final part of Section 2 revisits some of the questions about race and the body raised by *An Octoroon* but considers more specifically how the runaway slave serves as a prototype for a figure not fully recognized by society. Through an examination of Suzan-Lori Parks's *Father Comes Home from the Wars* (Parts 1, 2, and 3), I consider how enslaved people are not recognized as subjects, and, therefore, they offer a different genealogy of the body, particularly as it pertains to the body/mind hierarchy, gender, and sexuality. These genealogies call attention to theoretical developments about the body that emerge from different historical contexts and theoretical paradigms. How does the familial rearrangement in the play challenge traditional notions of family? How does Parks challenge what Sigmund Freud saw as primary psychic attachments (that is, between parent and child) and allow for alternative forms of desire to enliven the characters?   .

Section 3

The third and final section of *Bodies* explores theoretical developments that ask new questions about the body and its interpretation. These theories challenge normative strategies for reading the body. Theories of ecocriticism, transgender studies, and disability studies produce circuits of ideas that transform our understandings of the body by demonstrating its interconnection with other organisms. I examine Nick Dear's adaptation of Mary Shelley's nineteenth-century novel, *Frankenstein*, which again puts pressure on the singularity of the human experience as masterful rather than a part of a larger network, and I revisit *Father Comes Home from the Wars* (Parts 1, 2, and 3). With the precarity that climate crisis produces and the ways the body may be understood in relationship to other systems and structures (such as, economic, political, social, and cultural), the new areas of thought I survey here challenge in fresh ways the idea of the autonomous individual. While the theoretical frame throughout the book presumes the circulation of ideas about the body among humans, Section 3 considers also how nonhuman organisms contribute to understandings of the body. If nonhuman organisms contribute to the material conditions of humans' lives, one can easily understand how they inform the production of meaning as well. This section of the book takes seriously the idea of theories of the body that account for the body in a network of exchange with a wide array of organisms.

Pushing past understandings of a relay between body and mind as the basis of knowledge production, theories in ecocriticism, transgender studies, and disability studies call attention to how knowledge emerges between a range of human bodies as well as among species. Each one calls attention to the permeability of the body and the ways information flows through circuits. The aforementioned schools of thought account for human beings' limited control of the flow of power, posing a challenge to some of Foucault's earlier theories.

Transgender studies and disability studies in particular build on the instrumental work of women of color feminists and their understanding of how the position of the body may account for multiple and competing histories. In these schools of thought, individuals are multiply situated in relationship to history, power, and social contexts. The body then may be read in contesting and complicated ways depending on when and how it is perceived, and the nature of its interactions with other bodies and objects. Section 3 thus presents new theories of the body that explore interactions, flows, spills, and circuits to not only explode the hierarchy of the mind over the body, but to challenge the idea of the singular self-possessed human subject. The volume as a whole examines how theater contests, advances, and anticipates theories of the body as it offers complex understandings of meaning made through the relationships between theater artists and audiences.

SECTION ONE

Historical Approaches to Theater Theory

Introduction

This section offers a historical overview of how theater engages with theories of the body expressed in religious, cultural, social, familial, and communal practices and anticipates late twentieth-century theories of the body as a construction. I explore the theatrical conventions from the Medieval period to the twenty-first century that inform how bodies appear on stage. Although twentieth-century theorists offer useful frameworks to analyze the body on stage, theater makers have also implicitly offered theories of the body through its staging. Given how theater offers its own theories of the body, the first section of the book provides a historical overview of theater theories of the body and ends with an engagement with modern theorists whose work expands understandings of the body in theater studies. Throughout the section I question, what does the appearance and movement of the body on stage teach us about how history, power, culture, religion, and social context inform the materialization of the body? At the end of the section, my case study pairings draw attention to how contemporary playwright Branden Jacobs-Jenkins revises the medieval drama *Everyman* and the nineteenth-century play *The Octoroon* in his own work, *Everybody* (2017) and *An Octoroon* (2014) to highlight not only how theories of the body have changed over time but also to emphasize how theatrical devices help theorize those shifts.

Medieval Drama and the Christian Church

Calling attention to the body in pain, one of, if not the highest of, Christian holidays, Easter, commemorates the sacrifice of the son of God, Jesus Christ, through his hanging on a cross. Similar to animal sacrifices depicted in the Bible, the physical sacrifice of Jesus atones for sin and concretizes the subjugation of the body to the spirit. After three days, Jesus is resurrected, which affirms God's power to overcome death and the physical limitations of the body. It also situates the physical body as negligible. Jesus's crucifixion establishes the power of staging in the attribution of meaning to the body and the hierarchy of the soul over the body.

Staging continues to facilitate the communication of the religious value that subordinates the body to the soul and the mind. Jesus's death and resurrection serves as the cornerstone of Christianity and, therefore, periodically believers participate in the ritual of communion to remember the foundational sacrifice. During the ritual of communion as an act of consecration, Christians eat bread and drink wine, which symbolizes the sacrifice of Christ's body and blood, respectively. The consumption of the bread and the wine physically changes parishioners' bodies to remind them of their shared beliefs. In Christianity, communion, one of the seven sacraments, foregrounds the body's role in spiritual practice as a vessel to or roadblock for redemption. The other sacraments include baptism, confirmation, penance, anointing of the sick, marriage, and holy orders.

The performance of Christian rituals produces cultural reservoirs for religious communities and the theater in the medieval and modern periods. Medieval drama in particular draws attention to the tension between the belief that the body, or at least the body of Christ, can transmogrify and that the human body is a locus of sin that Christians must discipline. In addition, Christians also participate in penance—a self-punishment to right a wrong and receive absolution of sin that can include anything from a speech act to a physical punishment. The understanding that ideas, power structures, desires, histories, rituals, and belief systems materialize the body informs theatrical practices in the medieval period. How did medieval drama draw from religious practices and the staging of rituals and what are the implications of its conventions for a historical and theoretical understanding of the body?

In the medieval period, theater served communal purposes to teach lessons, impart beliefs, and draw individuals together. The theater served a pedagogical and ideological purpose. Community members, not professional artists, produced, acted in, and designed the productions and used physical enactment as one of the central sources of knowledge production (Enders 2019: 11). Medieval dramas detail stories from the bible beginning with creation and ending with the Last Judgment. As David Bevington describes, "In terms of staging, early morality plays make use of scaffolds and an open *platea* or 'place' as do other dramatic works of the period. ... Production in early morality drama, as in other forms of medieval open-air theater, makes use of colorful costuming, music, processions, bustling crowd scenes, and the like" (2012: 791–2). The plays often moved throughout the community, traveling through the streets and perhaps only garnering the passing glance of distracted neighbors. At the same time, the spectacles drew excited audiences to their stations to see a friend or coworker in a production. The integration of the pageants into everyday life produced deliberate and accidental audiences, confusing the bodies of passersby with those deliberately in representational roles. The theatrical productions of the medieval theater occurred alongside everyday life unfolding in open space and in institutions such as the church. As a result, the staging of the morality plays complemented other everyday activities that gave the body meaning, including labor practices and ritual enactments.

The participatory nature of theater in the medieval period calls attention to its similarity with other modes of staging and embodied actions including religious rituals. Medieval theater resembled other everyday forms of drama enacted in community:

> Following the historian Jacques Le Goff's seminal insight that medieval culture as a whole displayed a widespread tendency to theatricalize itself, it is fair to say that theatre was everywhere. Those undertaking to write its history must look to the myriad space where medieval people came together to revel in spectacles that had the potential to be repeated, formalized and committed to writing as the textual entity that we now dub "drama." We must look not only to scripted plays but to the multiple spectacular practices of multiple performers: to the poetry and songs of *scops*, bards and *jongleurs* (among the earliest "solo-performers"), to the tour-de-force oratorical displays of lawyers, priests, professors and politicians, and to such community festivities as folk dancing, processions and religious rituals. (Enders 2019: 2–3)

Enders's description offers a landscape of the performances that qualified as drama during the period. This multiplicity of presentation created a porousness around the implication of different forms of presentation for understanding individuals and their bodies.

Medieval drama challenges the distinction between the body in pain and the performing by putting actors at risk. Although pageants drew more attention to the stories of the characters than the individuals playing the roles, actors risked injury in reenacting violence, such as the crucifixion, which calls attention to the proximity of the character's pain and the actor's body in pain. In *The Body in Pain: The Making and Unmaking of the World*, Elaine Scarry calls attention to the singular experience of the body in pain. She writes, "Whatever pain achieves, it achieves in part through its unsharability" (1987: 4). Through the reenactment of violence, the pageants operate similarly to other religious rites, such as communion, that serve as acts of memory rather than representations of events. The pedagogical core of pageants suggest that even if the unfolding of the event impacts the body, resulting in pain, the impact serves as a reminder for the participant of the unshareable pain Jesus suffered, for example. The goal in medieval drama was not to become the character but rather to impart a story or a lesson for both the actors and audience alike (see Aronson-Lehavi 2019: 61). Medieval drama theorized the body for audiences and through actors.

Case Study: *Everyman*

Everyman (1510) weaves an allegorical tale of a figure personifying mankind who must confront Death and his inevitable physical demise (Bevington 2012: 940). Before being dragged to the grave, the eponymous Everyman has the opportunity to account for his good and bad deeds on Earth. He learns through his interactions with the characters he meets, Fellowship, Kindred, and Goods, that they will not accompany him on his spiritual journey. He does, however, also encounter Knowledge, Good Deeds, and Confession who help him partake of the sacraments in order to secure his redemption. The play emphasizes how the physical sacrifice that Jesus made on the cross to redeem mankind offers a precedent for Everyman's ability to secure his personal salvation by investing in his soul rather than his body.

In the opening exchange of the play between the Messenger and God, God sets the stage for a reckoning with Everyman that highlights the body as a source of corruption and pain. Although in Christian theology God only takes embodied form in his son, Jesus, the play offers a physical representation of the deity. He says, lamenting man's propensity to sin, "They fear not my rightwiseness, the sharp rod; My law that I shewed, when I for them died, They forget clean, and shedding of my blood red; I hanged between two, it cannot be denied; To get them life I suffered to be dead" (Ward 1995: 37). God laments that mankind has forgotten the brutality he suffered through the crucifixion. He says man has forgotten that the sacrifice of Jesus's blood made them clean (Bevington 2012: 941). The emphasis on physical discipline and sacrifice upholds the waywardness of the body as a source of trouble while also emphasizing, through the actor playing God, the proximity of the deity to humans in their suffering. Instead of devotion to God, man indulges in the seven deadly sins (pride, greed, wrath, envy, lust, gluttony, and sloth). The story of the crucifixion, the idea that God sent his son to earth in human form as a sacrifice to redeem mankind, affirms the hierarchy of the soul over the body. In this hierarchy, the body is aligned with sinful human desires and the soul becomes associated with transcendence. Human's denial of bodily desires and emotions draws them closer to God. At the same time, the body becomes the site for punishment, sacrifice, and discipline in the name of spiritual ascendance.

Medieval drama's references to and depiction of the crucifixion established a theory of the body as the flawed container for both mind and spirit. In this period, the staging of Christian allegories served to remind community members of the ability to shape the body into a more pious version of itself. In *Everyman* the central character's journey follows the doctrines of Christianity; his partaking of the sacraments enables his redemption, particularly his confession of wrongdoing and penance.

The physical punishment of the body with a "knotted scourge"—a multi-thong lash with knots on the end of each rope—seeks to mimic Jesus's suffering on the cross and draw attention to physical sacrifice as a means of spiritual redemption (Bevington 2012: 954). The physical pain caused by the knotted scourge mimics the torture that Jesus experienced and the sacrifice of the body as a means of redemption. The physical body in pain serves as currency to pay for man's sins in exchange for God's forgiveness. The sacrament of communion also serves to call attention to the disciplining of the flesh through ingesting food and drink that stands for the body and blood of Christ as a necessary step in obtaining spiritual transcendence but functions as a memory ritual rather than a physical penance that functions similarly to Christ's sacrifice. Although the Bible details following Jesus's crucifixion that no one else must die to pay for men's sins, the physical punishment serves as an act of penance that recalls Jesus's body in pain to not only punish the participant but to draw to his mind the sacrifice that Jesus made for him. Both acts—communion and penance—however, draw attention to the inherent theatricality of actual religious ritual and the similarity between dramatic and religious production during the period. *Everyman* establishes the similarities between religious rituals and theatrical drama in the Medieval period. The play represents religious rites to teach community members religious lessons through embodied practices and interactive learning.

Early Modern Theater and the Unreliable Sexual Body

Understandings of the body on and off stage in the early modern period (1400–1650) reflect a transition in European culture from primarily religious contexts for interpretation to an engagement with how economic and scientific changes during the period shifted readings of the body on and off stage. Similar to the medieval period, performance, both professional and quotidian, continued to be a space to work through, contest, and engage these developments. While the predominate view of the body would not fully shift from religious to secular terms until the eighteenth century (the Enlightenment period), Christianity's hold on the body in the Western world began to loosen by the late sixteenth century. Nevertheless, the common association of the early modern period with Shakespeare does not account for "the sustained importance, in the post-Reformation age, of religious theatre" (Henke 2019: 5). Particularly when "considered transnationally, Corpus Christi cycles and Passion plays flourish more in [this] historical period than in that of [the medieval period]" (Henke 2019: 5). Investment in theological readings of the body produced contestation over the implicit and overt displays of sexuality on- and offstage, which would gain steam as a result of economic and scientific developments. In the early modern period, what new theatrical conventions develop to produce theories of the body as the theater transitions from religious to secular worlds?

The development of capitalism as the primary economic structure in the Western world resulted in professionalization of theater: "Italy was both the birthplace of Western capitalism and the crucible of the professional actor (even as the early modern professional actor, across Europe, oddly straddled neo-feudal and proto-capitalist modes)" (Henke 2019: 4). As a result, theater began to shape the body as labor. Commercial theaters and national theaters developed in the sixteenth century. In these new spaces, however, the distinction we now make in amphitheaters between the professional work taking place onstage and the position of the consuming audience offstage did not adhere. More similar to a shift from the immersive theater of the medieval period to the clear distinctions between audience and actors in contemporary traditional theater, "The physical configurations and material conditions of public performance spaces in early modern Europe favoured the pressing together of bodies, enabling playgoers to brush up closely against each other, and to see and be seen at very close range by actors themselves" (Nicholson 2019: 60). While theater began to move toward a distinct separation between actors and audiences, rendering the performances onstage different from the acts that constituted the body in everyday life, in this period, the distinction, such as in Shakespeare's Globe Theatre, remained porous.

The professionalization of early modern theatrical experience coincided with developments in scientific knowledge of the body and called attention to how the theater served as a space to explore new ideas. Surgical techniques including "the development of clinical dissection, with its applications from medicine and surgery to the visual arts, practiced amidst clerical opposition in both private and public spaces—eventually in purpose-built 'anatomy theatres' such as those of Padua and Leiden—led to growing rejection of the traditional Galenic 'one-sex, two-genders' model, along with an analytic treatment of the body 'in parts'" (Nicholson 2019: 52; see also Schleiner 2000). New scientific knowledge of the body destabilized the authority of the church and the hierarchy of men over women. Scientists reversed the understanding that women and men shared the same sex organs. They realized women had distinct organs and not simply had interior versions of male anatomy.

The destabilization of traditional beliefs about sexual anatomy coincided with new expressions of gender in performance. According to Eric Nicholson:

In the late fifteenth to sixteenth centuries, masculinity was on prominent show, through the use of close-fitting and sometimes parti-coloured stockings, leading the attracted eye towards an often upward-thrusting codpiece. Femininity was likewise fashioned and refashioned in exhibitionist terms, as hooped farthingales became wider, heeled shoes became taller, fabrics more expensive and elaborately woven as well as embroidered, and close-fitting bodices and corsets tighter, with protruding triangular "plackets" or pointed "stomachers" that directed gazes towards the (covered) female pudenda. (2019: 53)

The adornment, although perhaps not conceptualized as so, offered an early distinction between gender and sex. The tightly fitted clothing may have functioned more to conceal than reveal, given the common practice of younger men playing women in productions. The stage continued to serve as a place to explore and comment on the body through ideological work and the ongoing circulation of medieval pageants that displayed the suffering body and it began, as described above, to experiment with costuming to offer another layer of meaning to the body.

Case Study: William Shakespeare's *Twelfth Night, Or What You Will*

The plot of William Shakespeare's comedy *Twelfth Night, Or What You Will*, experiments with the fluidity of gender roles through the cross-dressing of the central figure Viola as Cesario but contains the threat of such fluidity of performance in the everyday through the play's resolution in heterosexual marriage. Through acts of cross-dressing, the play creates love triangles that bend the protocols for desire and depend on the erasure of reproduction (and, therefore, inheritance) as a concern. Establishing the theater as a site for play that will ultimately uphold predominate beliefs about the body, the end of the play affirms heterosexual marriage as mechanism for the rightful transfer of property through inheritance. The play opens with Viola shipwrecked and separated from her twin brother. Viola assumes that her brother is dead and decides to "conceal" who she is and present herself as a "eunuch" so that the Duke Orsino will employ her (1.2.54 and 1.2.57). In order to affect the presentation of Cesario, Viola must shift her physical appearance, not simply in terms of clothing but also stance, gait, and interactions. Consider social expectations for how cisgender men sit and stereotypically take up space versus how cisgender women tend to cross their legs at the knee or ankle. Women also tend to have higher voices, a pitch Viola would abandon as Cesario. Unexpectedly, Orsino tasks

Viola with helping him court Lady Olivia. In the interim, Viola falls in love with Orsino and Oliva falls in love with Viola/Cesario. Viola must then figure out how to satisfy her desire and duties. In the play, the lovers demonstrate the flexibility of gender roles in theatrical production during the period. The end of the play reveals the identities of the players and results in a heteronormative resolution for the star-crossed lovers. Nevertheless, cross-dressing allows for the circulation of queer desire through gender performance without upsetting the centrality of the body's role in the circulation of wealth through marriage and procreation.

As Carol Thomas Neely explains in *Distracted Subjects*, critics question the stakes of triangulating desire in *Twelfth Night*. Neely summarizes: "*Twelfth Night* subordinates both women and erotic possibility." Referencing scholar Jean Howard, Neely continues, "Viola's 'properly feminine subjectivity' makes her masculine attire non-threatening while the genuinely unruly woman, Olivia, is humiliated and punished by 'being made to fall in love with the cross dressed Viola,' leading to the 'containment of gender and class insurgency'" (2004: 115–16). Ultimately, cross-dressing in the *Twelfth Night* does not upset the conventional function of the body as the conduit for the transmission of property. As the play concludes, Neely points out that Olivia's offer to pay for Orsino's wedding to Viola/Cesario shifts her relationship to both of them. She explains, "[Olivia's] offer… generate[s] his explicit offer of marriage to Cesario and the giving of his hand: 'Here is my hand; you shall from this time be I Your master's mistress…' But Olivia concludes the line—'A sister; you are she'—translating her affection for Viola/Cesario into a new configuration. Hence the play that begins in the household of Orsino ends at Olivia's; she displaces the Duke as the primary authority figure in Illyria" (2004: 121). The play does disrupt gender conventions by challenging what social spaces different bodies may occupy.

A practice shared by prostitutes and boy actors alike, cross-dressing served as a way to entice onlookers and simultaneously, in different contexts, to police women's bodies: "Cross-dressing was widely practiced by prostitutes both on the continent and in England as a means of exciting clients' desire … Likewise, the cross-dressing boy actors of the stage were often charged with homosexual prostitution, though opinions on this subject ranged from the puritanical to the tolerant and even indulgent" (Nicholson 2019: 60–1). The use of boys to play women on English stage helped to cement women's position offstage even as she garnered the title Diva throughout the continent. Labor practices informed who could play a woman, so professional theaters teemed with "talented teenage male actors" (Nicholson 2019: 65). The grappling over women's roles (economic, social, and cultural) would continue to unfold during the Enlightenment period as the idea of a thinking subject became central to debates about the human.

The Enlightenment Period: Mind and Body

In Western medieval and early modern traditions, the body served sometimes as an inconvenient and other times as a useful container for the mind and soul. The distinction between inconvenient and useful often hinged on how the body could further social distinctions of station or sex. Distinctions between bodies correlated to social positions and one's proximity to God. In the transition from the early modern period to the Enlightenment, theater artists continued to wrangle with the secularization of the form. Instead of establishing the hierarchy of the soul over the body, Enlightenment theater affirmed the hierarchy of the mind over the body. Enlightenment theater artists, however, presumed the white male body as *the* body, rendering his experience universal.

The prioritizing of the white male body followed theater artists understanding of a universal audience. At the same time,

Enlightenment theories, most notably those of René Descartes, articulated a burgeoning understanding of individualism, which specified the diversity of a theatrical production's meaning based on its reception. On the one hand, "the classical theory of tragedy conceptually relies on a universally shared experience of pity and fear for its audience," on the other hand, "the nascent, modern understanding of subjectivity fundamentally disavows this possibility because of the individualistic nature of the emotions" (Gobert 2013: 52). The distinction between universalism and burgeoning individualism has implications not only for the actors on stage but also for the audience because it points to fundamental understandings about sources of knowledge and the flexibility of social position. Rather than being born into a certain position, the idea of individual subjectivity suggested one had the opportunity to act in furtherance of or opposition to their birth. How does the shifting understanding of agency inform theories of the body in the Enlightenment period for actors as well as audiences?

In the *Republic,* Plato establishes theater as metaphor for the internal workings of the human mind that continues to hold sway in philosophical writing into the eighteenth century. As R. Darren Gobert explains:

> mental activity has been likened to theatrical spectacle since antiquity, and by philosophers and theorists of quite different persuasions. Descartes himself may have given the metaphor particular traction when he envisioned a performance space in the pineal gland, where, as on opening night, "it all comes together." I borrow the phrase from philosopher Daniel C. Dennett, whose immodestly titled *Consciousness Explained* derides this pervasive understanding as "The Cartesian Theater"—an ersatz image with appeal to "crowds ... transfixed by an illusion," not unlike Plato's enslaved spectators. Dennett speaks of audiences; Hume, of postures being struck; Plato, of sight lines. But the strenuous labor and pleasing tactility of the theatrical endeavor remain unrecognized. (2013: 2)

The philosophical tradition of depicting theater as a display of interiority does not allow for an interplay between body and mind but rather subordinates the body to the mind. The use of the body as a means of expression relegates theater to a lesser art form. It also positions the body, through its appearance on stage and ability to transform before spectators, as screen or site of illusion that distracts from higher ethical, moral, or religious concerns (see Cheng 2013). Note the shift from theatrical display as a reflection of religious beliefs about and through the body in the medieval period to its status as a distraction from higher orders of concern.

Although many scholars associate Descartes with affirming the hierarchy of the mind over the body, Gobert's *The Mind-Body Stage* establishes an alternative perspective to the one ingrained by the philosopher's most often-cited assertion in *Discourse on Method*, "I think, therefore I am (je pense, donc je suis)." Gobert suggests that in the Enlightenment period, Descartes's late writing acknowledges the now well-established understanding of an interplay between body and mind that occurs individually and distinctly for each performer and spectator. The physical experience of playing a role produces sensations that function as a source of knowledge, which informs future actions.

Alternatively, the physical display may not align at all with the interiority of the actor. Instead of functioning as a metaphor, the display may serve as evidence of training and will. The actor's ability to convince an audience of an emotional state without necessarily inhabiting the emotional state draws attention to expectations for bodily display and staging as much as they point to a disruption in the Enlightenment period about the relationship between the body and the mind and the body as source of emotional expression.

At the same time that philosophers began to reconsider the complex relationship between the body and the mind, the understanding of sex as a category of difference began to shift. Until the eighteenth century, theorists understood "male and female bodies" "as being variants of one body type placed at different points on a vertical continuum. Within the 'one-sex' model, sexual difference had been a matter of degree and sex had been a sociological rather than an ontological category" (Brooks 2019: 57). During the period, however, a dualistic model took hold. The idea of the incommensurability of male and female bodies emerged. They "were understood to be anatomically and qualitatively different." As a result, "the sexed body became the primary site of identity and difference, and was drawn on to determine and constrain men's and women's social roles and behaviours, economic activities, and sexual desires" (Brooks 2019: 57). Although the enlightenment period inaugurated the fuller incorporation of women as professional actors, the renaissance practice of cross-dressing persisted, but with new implications given the evolving understanding of sex. The latter half of the eighteenth century saw reduction of these male travesty roles and a limitation of them to secondary characters "such as the nurses in Henry Nevil Payne's tragedy *The Fatal Jealousy* (1672), and in Otway's adaptation of *Romeo and Juliet*, *Caius Marius* (1680); the landlady in Thomas Scott's *The Mock Marriage* (1695); Mrs. Fardingale in Richard Steele's *The Funeral* (1701); and the first trull in Thomas Shadwell's *Humours of the Army* (1713)" (Brooks 2019: 58). Women playing men on stage, conversely, had the opportunity to express embodiment unrestricted by newly forming prohibitions on womanhood and the long skirts and petticoats that helped to sustain them.

Although conventions and power dynamics prescribe forms of expression and their reception, the Enlightenment period marked a turn toward contemporary understandings of interiority formed through physical repetition and the flow of experience working to produce understanding and attachments. Gobert explains,

Two central aspects of this general picture need to be highlighted. The first is that, in the Cartesian model, habituation shapes all of our actions and passions, starting with the impressions received in utero and rendered increasingly complex with each and every experience; as I walk differently as I age, so do I think differently, and so do I love differently. Significantly, just as the muscles of every subject-body are different (and not just in response to different stimuli). The second is that some of this habituation is not only beyond the subject's control but also deliberately clouds her view of her own agency: the passions, after all, take their name from a Latin etymon meaning "to suffer" and are so called because they happen *to* us. They are caused by movements in the body, but we cannot perceive the interior workings that constitute their proximate cause. (2013: 94)

This flow of ideas, however, only applied to white male bodies, and not to women or people of color. The idea of liberal humanism assumed white male actors. While the Cartesian model does not fully account for the structural impact of social implications that adheres in postmodern theories of performance as articulated by Judith Butler, Fred Moten, and Richard Schechner, it grounds an understanding of movement as a source of knowledge that adheres overtime and that occurs individually. Questions about who qualifies as an individual subject and therefore a source of knowledge will predominate the age of empire and complicate understanding of the body. The shifting perception of individuality also allowed for the emergence of the celebrity actor who had particular cache in communicating a mood, scenario, or experience.

Age of Empire: The Circulation of Racialized Bodies

Marked by the expansion of territory through slavery and colonization, the age of empire laid the foundation for Europe's influence in the Americas, Africa, and the Caribbean.

In this period, theories about race qualified and disqualified individuals from appearing in the courts or society as rights holding subjects. The age of empire marked the expansion of individualism and race-based conquest, establishing white people as uniquely qualified to function as social and dramatic actors. Similar to the early modern period, however, theater emerged as a site to test embodied hierarchies and social evaluations of the body. Enlightenment theater establishes the hierarchy of mind over the body based on scientific advancements. In the age of empire, law advances a hierarchy of white bodies over Black bodies.

Race was believed to be in the blood and thus informs theories of the body and complicates understandings of gender. The US Supreme Court affirmed the long-held belief in race as biologically determined in the *Plessy v. Ferguson* (1896) ruling. In 1890, Homer Plessy joined a group of concerned citizens that sought to challenge the State of Louisiana Act 111 that required separate accommodations on railway cars for Black and white people. The group decided that Plessy, who appeared white but had African ancestry, would purchase a ticket for and board the whites-only car and then reveal himself as Black so that he would be thrown off. The group hoped to expose the lack of scientific or legal basis for Act 111. Eventually, the case did come before the Supreme Court, which upheld the constitutionality of segregation and the illegality of Homer Plessy, who was one-eighth Black, riding in an all-white railway car in Louisiana:

> Homer Plessy's act of strategic passing, ironically dedicated to the demise of racial discrimination, was read by the Supreme Court as an act of appropriation, as an unqualified theft of an identity imagined as property—as that which is properly and privately owned by a "legitimate" white subject ... it was precisely in the name of identity *as* property that the Plessy case waged its battle against segregation and in the name of "natural" ownership that the Plessy claim was denied. (Robinson 1996: 238)

The court case affirms how physical appearance enabled one to move in space, drawing attention to how courts defined and regulated the Black body.

In the United States, separate but equal remained the law of the land until the Supreme Court's 1954 ruling in *Brown v. the Board of Education* found that separate schools were inherently unequal. Although *Plessy v. Ferguson* established the legal framework for the colloquial standard "the one drop rule" (which finds that if you have one drop of Black blood, you qualify as Black), it also highlights the danger and anxiety raised by individuals who did not appear to be Black even though they may have had African ancestry. The basis of scientific racism depended on a clear physical differentiation between white and Black people. As a result, Plessy's ability to buy the first-class train ticket, board the train, and enjoy the privilege of a white passenger undercut the logic that one's biology determined one's actions, and therefore draws attention to policing as a function of the body's appearance. In fact,

> Only when a spectator adopts the presumptive mechanisms that "read" a racially indeterminate subject as a legible social identity can a subject truly be said to pass ... In an economy of presumed legibility (you are what you look like), the successful passer only disappears from view insofar as s/he appears (to her reader) to be the category into which s/he passed. (Robinson 1996: 241)

In fact, Plessy does not become Black for the other passengers on the train until he announces himself as such, which begs the question: what in fact qualifies him as Black?

On both sides of the Atlantic, the uncertainty about the scientific basis for racial hierarchies that abolitionists (i.e. Toussaint Louverture, Harriet Tubman, John Brown, William Lloyd Garrison, Frederick Douglass, David Walker, Nat Turner, William Wells Brown, and Ellen and William Craft) produced emerged in representation on stage. From Victorian pantomimes to American minstrel shows, the stage featured the physical transformation of figures. In *Bodies in Dissent*, Daphne Brooks explains:

> Both the American minstrel show and Victorian spectacular pantomimes rode waves of curiously similar cultural obsessions with physical metamorphoses; the exhibition of (in)authentically transfigured and socially "deviant" bodies—white men masquerading as black caricatures— radically recalls the pantomime narratives' emphasis on a surplus corporeality and superabundant representation as central thematic and visual attractions of the productions. (Brooks 2006: 26)

Trans-Atlantic slavery sought to reduce Black people to laboring bodies with the effort of their work functioning as a surplus. In addition, Black people produced "surplus corporeality," or Black bodies as property that functioned to produce more property in the persons of their children. The idea of the Black body being for the use of white people informed representation on stage in the age of empire and understandings of the body in social and legal contexts.

Case Study: Boucicault's *The Octoroon*

One of the most influential plays of the period, Dion Boucicault's *The Octoroon*, draws from the theatrical conventions of the nineteenth century to intervene in theories of the body as physiologically distinct depending on race. The title references a person that is one-eighth Black. The play depicts a transition in the ownership of the Terrebonne plantation in Louisiana. Nephew of the estate's deceased patriarch, George Peyton, returns home thinking he will inherit Terrebonne since Judge Peyton passed away without any children. George and his aunt, Mrs. Peyton, learn, however, that Judge Peyton mortgaged Terrebonne and left it vulnerable to collectors upon his passing. Although the Judge had also given written notice that upon his death his daughter, Zoe, an octoroon, would be free, under US law his debts enabled the reclamation of her as property as well. Her racial status not only disqualified her from inheritance, it barred her father from freeing her as well. Overlaying the central plot, a scheming upstart, Jacob M'Closky, finds a way to purchase Zoe. In order to do so, he must prevent the Peytons from receiving a letter that confirms the payment of a settlement large enough to save Terrebonne. In intercepting the letter, M'Closky kills another enslaved person, Paul, and pins the murder on the play's Native American character, Wahnotee. Technology, however, foils M'Closky's plot because as he kills Paul, the new camera that the overseer of Terrebonne purchased captures him in the act. M'Closky ends up paying for his wrongdoing but, as I will explain later in this section, the fate of Zoe shifts between the American and British production of the play.

Boucicault's play explores excess—excessive histories, bodies, nations, families—in order to distinguish it from the norm. By presenting excessive bodies, histories, and family relationships, melodramas like *The Octoroon* give expression to narratives that the regulatory norms that govern civil society repress and therefore they cannot fit within the confines of the quotidian. The primitivist representation of Wahnotee, for example, evidences a racial, political, social, and historical imaginary that motivates desires and supports social and cultural mandates, reinforcing what nineteenth-century audiences deem taboo, such as race mixing, and what they regarded as socially acceptable, including white men playing Black and brown people on stage. The white body could represent anyone because white people defined race in the law. Melodrama as a form serves this cultural purpose of giving expression to those unspeakable things in "polite" society that must remain absent presences, "hiding" in the wings and haunting American culture. Although theater explored taboo topics like interracial desire, it did so through white actors to limit the threat of the imagined world slipping into the quotidian one. As the play depicts, George and Zoe cannot marry because she is one-eighth Black, and in the production of the play, a white actress plays Zoe, depicting the exclusion of Black people from legal systems and the stage, even if they appear white. The casting begs the question, as does the play, what renders Zoe Black and who determines her racial status?

Key features of melodrama include excess in expression of emotion as well as in terms of situations. Characters returning from the dead, the hero arriving just in time to foil a fiendish plot, or the materialization of a conveniently lost and now suddenly found family member, melodrama thrives on pushing realism to its breaking point only to reestablish order by its end. Resolution in melodrama requires the promise that good will be victorious and evil will be punished. Melodrama draws us in, no matter how ridiculous, with the promise to replicate the given social order. That promise secures us for the rollercoaster ride of emotions and scenarios that we gladly witness in order to return with strict divisions, clear categorizations, and explicit differentiations—Black and white, man and women, self and other.

Although melodrama requires by play's end a reestablished social order through a stark and decisive contrast between right and wrong, Zoe's fate in Boucicault's play posed a problem. For American audiences her fate reflected Boucicault's stance on the impending US Civil War, while British audiences understood it as a referendum on the 1833 abolition of slavery throughout the Empire. To emphasize Zoe's tragic case, in both the American and British production of the play a white woman played the role wearing blackface makeup. The makeup emphasizes Zoe's physical difference even though plot hinges on George's initial inability to tell that his beloved is Black. The production therefore makes physical appearance adhere to beliefs about racial difference being visible in contradiction to the play.

She therefore only disrupted the idea of Blackness; she did not require audiences to find sympathy for an actual Black person in order to enjoy the play. As Zoe states to rebuff George's love for her, one drop of Black blood taints her and renders her property. She laments,

> that is the ineffaceable curse of Cain. Of the blood that feeds my heart, one drop in eight is black—bright read as the rest may be, that one drop poisons all the blood. Those seven bright drops give me love like yours, hope like yours—ambition like yours—life hung with passions like dew-drops on the morning flowers; but the one black drop gives me despair, for I'm an unclean thing-forbidden by the laws—I'm an Octoroon! (2014: 43)

Zoe's description of her social position reinstalls a Biblical understanding of social order to support racial hierarchies and the understanding of Black people as property. Her physical description segments her body. Although Zoe appeared in the US and English productions of the play as a lady, separate from the other enslaved characters, her status hinges on misapprehension according to the law. Her body in the play becomes a primary site of evidence and misinformation at the same time. In the US production of the play, to resolve Zoe's unjust fate, she commits suicide before learning that Terrebonne will be saved. In the British production, George and Zoe run away together to wed.

The description of Zoe as Judge Peyton's daughter and George's star-crossed (in the US version) love calls attention to how the individual mixed-race body serves as an allegory for the nation state in the age of empire. In US history, Sally Hemings (1773–1835), a woman enslaved by President Thomas Jefferson and mother to several of his children, represents what is referred to as a "ghost family," the family produced from the common practice of white slave owners impregnating enslaved women. In these contexts, enslaved women did not have any legal rights of bodily autonomy or ones that they could exercise on behalf of their children. As a result, the slave owner not only affirmed his Enlightenment belief in the subordination of the body to the mind but also his subordination of any and all racialized bodies to the will and whim of the white mind. This practice flew in the face of America's purported egalitarian democracy that had been established in part by Jefferson. The hypocrisy at the heart of American slavery created a fissure that threatened, and continues to threaten, the national body.

The auction scene that closes Act 3 fuses the spectacle of slavery with generic conventions of nineteenth-century melodrama to heighten the feeling of injustice and to draw attention to the dubious character of the body as a fixed source of material evidence. As Brooks suggests, "Boucicault's innovations and investment in the culture of spectacular melodrama are inextricably linked to his production of the body of the 'tragic octoroon' on stage, and indeed this kind of use of the spectacle had far-reaching effects on the ways in which race and the body were subsequently performed in the transatlantic culture" (2006: 32). This auction scene in particular featured the display of a white actor playing a mixed-race figure who, according to the stage directions, stands on a table for the bidders' examination. While many of the planters agree to allow Zoe to return to being the property of the Peyton family, M'Closky finally exercises his legal rights to purchase and outbids all the other planters to win Zoe. The presentation of Zoe in the scene, using the conventions of slavery, serves to establish her as chattel, but the world of the play challenges such easy categorizations through its casting, particularly given the convention in melodrama that "the actor's body speak and perform a particular notion of 'truth' that was, in some cases, deemed more valuable than the character's discursive expression" (Brooks 2006: 37). In a similar way to how *Plessy v. Ferguson* relied on the verisimilitude of the physical body, melodrama understood the veracity of visible signs. *The Octoroon* drew those sign systems into question in order to heighten the emotional and tragic aspects of the drama. The play did so, however, using a white actress to play Zoe. The casting affirms the ability of the white body to encompass all experience and the inability of the Black person to physically take up stage space.

Modern Theories of the Body: Staging Reconsideration

Through the use of different theatrical forms, contemporary African American playwright Branden Jacob-Jenkins engages with and revises theories of the body. I will look now at two plays by Jacob-Jenkins—*Everybody* and *An Octoroon*—to show how he adapts and revises dramas of earlier periods to consider how earlier conceptions of the body inform contemporary theories. These plays engage with other questions raised by their predecessor texts, most expertly and thoughtfully about how genre shapes the body in theatrical presentation. Both of his plays reflect the shift from understandings of the body residing in the materiality of the organism—being biologically determined—to late-twentieth-century theories of post-structuralism (Butler, Bhabha, Derrida) that present understandings of the body as the accumulation of information rather than predetermined. For example, the same physical body would be categorized as Black in the United States, colored in South Africa, and Portuguese in Portugal based on historical conventions and cultural customs that inform perceptions of the same individual. Yet these distinctions leave some room for the individual to maneuver by interceding in the historical narrative or writing a new chapter of history as Jacob-Jenkins's plays show us. Similarly, the increasingly common practice of articulating one's preferred pronouns, either in an introduction or on a nametag, recoups the power of an onlooker assuming one's gender and resituates identification in the hands of the individual.

As I explain elsewhere, individual's intercession into performances of gender or race may have momentary impact, but in order to sustain power they must be repeated. I write:

> Performance theorist Judith Butler explores the interplay between performance—"twice-behaved behavior"—and performativity—the crystallized, hailing, regulatory power of identity categories and social positions (woman, man, Euro-American, African-American, teacher, athlete, mother, father, child). Over time, performances usually function to reinforce normative identities, by which I mean modes of presentation that reinforce social expectations based on race, gender, class, and sexual hierarchies (white, cisgender, heterosexual). Nevertheless, performance and performativity exist in a reciprocal relationship that shifts the meaning of each over time. (Colbert 2016b: 401–2)

Although in post-structuralist thought theorists present identity as a construct—a historical artifact consolidated through repeated actions over time—it functions as a structure that houses dominant desires and imperial power relations.

In *Discipline and Punish*, Michel Foucault describes how the modern body formed in relationship to power structures and, differentiating between the medieval and modern body, he explains:

> The moment that saw the transition from historico-ritual mechanisms for the formation of individuality to the scientifico-disciplinary mechanisms, when the normal took over from the ancestral, and measurement from status, thus substituting for the individuality of the memorable man that of the calculable man, that moment when the sciences of man became possible is the moment when a new technology of power and a new political anatomy of the body were implemented. (1995: 193)

Developments in scientific understandings of the body were used to enforce power for white Western men and punish other kinds of bodies.

In the late twentieth century, theorists began to conceptualize identity as a social construction, understanding race, gender, and sexuality as discursive categories that drew their social force from their historical use and application. Although Simone de Beauvoir wrote in *The Second Sex* (1949) "One is not born, but rather becomes, a woman," general acceptance of the idea that identity expressed social and historical conventions instantiated through repeated behavior and rhetoric did not take hold until much later. Best known is Butler's work in *Bodies That Matter* defining the body as a historical, discursive, and social construction. She writes:

> what constitutes the fixity of the body, its contours, its movements, will be fully material, but materiality will be rethought as the effect of power, as power's most productive effect. And there will be no way to understand "gender" as a cultural construct which is imposed upon the surface of matter, understood either as "the body" or its given sex. Rather, once "sex"itself is understood in its normativity, the materiality of the body will not be thinkable apart from the materialization of that regulatory norm. "Sex" is, thus, not simply what one has, or a static description of what one is: it will be one of the norms by which the "one" becomes viable at all, that which qualifies a body for life within the domain of cultural intelligibility. (1993: 2)

Thus the legibility of the body within cultural contexts becomes the basis for one's viability within those contexts, for one's humanity. While Butler carefully explains that "materiality will be rethought as the effect of power," regulatory norms support holding matter in place (Foucault's idea of discipline). The perception of or desire for impermeability, for a static, fixed body, produces materiality and forms the imaginary borders of the body. But bodies are porous and, against all desires, nevertheless remain in motion and in common.

Post-structuralists do not suggest that biological differences do not influence individual or collective identities at all. Rather, they argue that the meaning we ascribe to differences (in terms of body parts and types, skin tone, etcetera) emerges from culturally and socially specific systems of signification, or meaning-production, and are hence contextual, and not innate or fixed. Thus, even though we are born with specific types of bodies and corporeal traits, post-structuralists maintain, these do not carry meaning in and of themselves but only acquire differentiated significance within existing, hierarchal systems of meaning and value.

Post-structuralist notions of identity open up opportunities to challenge and destabilize established hierarchies of meaning and being. Even if there is such a thing as differently sexualized bodies, birth does not produce differences between men and women, but rather the contexts into which they are born that introduce boys and girls to certain modes of appropriate behavior while outlawing other ways of being in the world. The social convention to dress baby boys in blue and to make baby girls wear pink establishes an ostensibly minor, and yet significant, protocol for traditional (and future) gender practices. And this is not the only way in which infantile bodies are marked by social and cultural convention: class, race, nationality, and ethnicity are equally significant structures to attribute meaning to nascent personalities. Such structures do not operate independently, but each exerts its force in shifting configurations on the human organism on its way to become a socioculturally recognizable subject: "According to poststructuralism, subjectivity is never monolithic or fixed, but decentered, and constantly thrown into process by the very competing discourses through which identity might be claimed" (Dolan in Martin 1996: 96). Post-structuralism provides the opportunity to rethink the structures that govern gender hierarchies, but also complicates the idea of a "collective experience" shared by women across all sociocultural domains and fields of knowledge. If an essential notion of womanhood had provided the basis for the emergence of women's movement and collective action, it also reinforced a reified female identity that denied the experiences of women of color, as well as those of poor, queer, trans, and transnational women. A post-structuralist approach to all forms of identity as multiple, complex, and potentially conflicting helps to overcome such exclusions.

While "gender" and "race" both manifest as social categories through repeated behaviors and rhetorical conventions that are inflected by history and power, the histories that govern each term differ as do the temporal experience of each category. In the Introduction to *Race and Performance after Repetition*, cowritten with Douglas Jones and Shane Vogel, I explain often racialized performances "toggle between past and present" (2020: 4). We borrow language from

> theater phenomenologist Alice Rayner, who invites us to think of time (in relation to performance) not as "a series of points or a line or even a circle" that may repeat or recur, but as "a modality that dismantles fixed subjects and objects and turns past, present and future into ways of manners of attention." In thinking of time as a manner of attention, time appears less as a shape or direction or a reference point—something to be repeated—and more as a mood and an existential-phenomenological structure. Time, she writes, "puts attention on those things that matter most to care or concern." (2020: 20)

Case Study: Branden Jacob-Jenkins's *An Octoroon*

Jacobs-Jenkins's *An Octoroon* reworks the conventions of melodrama to trouble the legibility of the body and the structures that inform our engagement with it. Drawing from the history of *The Octoroon*, discussed above, Jacobs-Jenkins's play examines theatrical casting practices that racialize bodies in order to call into question our understanding of how material histories imbue theatrical production historically and in the present. This play begins with a confession from a figure named BJJ. He discloses, "Hi, everyone. I'm a 'black playwright.' I don't know exactly what that means, but I'm here to tell you a story" (2015: 7). African American poet and thinker Langston Hughes expertly distilled this historic struggle in his essay "The Negro and the Racial Mountain" (1926), concluding,

> We younger Negro artists who create now intend to express our individual dark-skinned selves without fear or shame. If white people are pleased we are glad. If they are not, it doesn't matter. We know we are beautiful. And ugly too. The tom-tom cries and the tom-tom laughs. If colored people are pleased we are glad. If they are not, their displeasure doesn't matter either. We build our temples for tomorrow, strong as we know how, and we stand on top of the mountain, free within ourselves.

The specificity of the designation "black playwright" points to the overdetermination of race in American culture. Even if by the time of the world premiere of *An Octoroon* by Soho Rep (New York, 2014) the idea of racial meaning as biologically determined had been widely debunked, the circulation of race has still remained linked inextricably to the body, making its material appearance a predetermining category.

The play depicts how this materiality of the body animates race by deploying the now-dated practice of racial signification through face paint, most derisively associated with blackface, and by engaging contemporary conversations about nontraditional casting. The opening scene consists of BJJ rehearsing an exchange that he had with his therapist in response to her assertion that they "find a way to deal with [his] low-grade depression" (2015: 7). As a result of their conversation, BJJ decides to adapt Boucicault's *The Octoroon*. Everything begins to fall into place until, as the play tells us,

"All the white guys quit. And then I couldn't find any whiter guys to play any of the white guy parts, because they felt it was too 'melodramatic'" (2015: 8). After an exploration of whether BJJ's racial bias caused the white people to leave the show, the therapist suggests colorblind casing, but that in this case BJJ would play all the parts he needs. The convention of nontraditional casting emerged in the 1960s and began to take up steam in the 1980s in response to the dearth of diversity in theatrical production and this practice, most commonly associated with casting people of color in roles normally associated with white actors, emerged as a programmatic response to people of color's disenfranchisement in regional theaters. More recently, nontraditional casting has caused controversy when white actors have been cast in roles specified as people of color (see Eyring). One would be erroneous to see the two practices as equivalent. As Brandi Wilkins Catanese notes in *The Problem of the Color[blind]*, "Harry Newman, then-executive director of the Non-Traditional Casting Project, wrote in 1989 of a 'four-year study by Actors' Equity Association completed in January 1986 [that] revealed that over 90 percent of all professional theatre produced in [the US] ... was stage with all-Caucasian casts" (2011: 10–11). Economic and social conditions inform the impact of artistic practices on actors' bodies. Therefore, when *An Octoroon* presents the challenges of a Black playwright offering a nuanced representation of race on stage, he does so cognizant of the history of white people easily assuming the roles of Black and Indigenous people on stage (blackface and redface performances) and the hard-fought battles of people of color to play any roles at all.

Ayanna Thompson's "Practicing a Theory/Theorizing a Practice: An Introduction to Shakespearean Colorblind Casting" (2006) traces the history of casting in US productions of Shakespeare, noting the impulse toward inclusion met resistance when companies did not account for audience reception. Locating the cultural currency that actors may access when cast in the Bard's work, Thompson draws attention to how Joseph Papp's New York Shakespeare Festival disrupted casting norms. In response to calls for the loosening of segregation in theaters, Papp created "a truly integrated theater that practiced colorblind casting" (2006: 4). The first wave of the practice held that the most qualified actor should play the role, requiring audiences to differentiate between the performer and the part. This had limited effect, depending on the circuits of relation in the play and the role itself. In particular, audiences have proven less game to accept colorblind casting when the play includes family members that are not cast of the same race and when productions have featured Black actors, they are far more often in supporting roles than leads. Thompson compares the reception of James Earl Jones as King Lear in 1973 with Black daughters to David Oyelowo cast in 2000 as King Henry but without Black children. The tension, as Thompson explains, not only points to the complexity of reception, but also to the difficulty in mapping ideas about gender performance onto racial ones.

The political and aesthetic challenges of colorblind casting differ from those of actors playing multiple roles, a strategy often adopted in an effort to reduce the size of the cast and cut costs. In *An Octoroon* BJJ also plays two white men, George and M'Closky, casting that blurs the line between racialized roles and those of hero and villain typical in a melodrama. BJJ's ability to embody the play's force of evil as well as its figuration of good calls into question the purported universalization of themes in the play and Boucicault's alternation of the ending once the play relocated from the United States to England. It also functions to comedic effect when the stage direction calls for George to attack M'Closky at the end of Act 3, "*George rushes M'Closky/himself, who draws his knife. They scuffle elaborately—the actor literally wrestling with himself*" (2015: 54). This shows that the force that threatens Zoe and the plantation as a whole is the same force that defends them.

The opening scene devolves and accelerates from the decision that BJJ will play George and M'Closky, intensifying in tone (there is a base-heavy soundtrack in the background that increases volume throughout) and through misdirection. BJJ reveals to the audience, "Just kidding. I don't have a therapist. I can't afford one. You people are my therapy" and then, according to the stage directions, "*BJJ gets into whiteface— possibly tries to cover his entire body with it*" (2015: 9). This confession serves to situate the theater as a space to work through traumatic racial histories. The play establishes a set of given circumstances only to unsettle them and resituate the audience's relationship to them, much as it wants to do with the material associations of race and the body. *An Octoroon* punctuates the act of disruption and reorientation through its use of whiteface which should conjure images of another popular nineteenth-century genre, minstrelsy. BJJ's transformation of his body through the use of white paint, however, does not have the same violent and derisive social history as the use of blackface by animating the ways Black people circulated through economies of substitution and exchange. Minstrelsy featured white characters in black face paint that stood in for their perceptions of Black people, producing an exchange that never approximates Black people but rather displays racial fantasies. BJJ's solution to white actors' unwillingness to participate in his adaptation draws whiteness into the logics of exchange that underpinned slavery. In so doing, he suggests that the disposability of the laboring body may have been a designation historically associated with Blackness but that it has crept into the economy of many artists in the twenty-first century.

The play calls attention to the idea of labor in an exchange between two enslaved characters: Minnie and Dido. In *An Octoroon*, unlike its precursor, these women play a more significant role. With advice laced with twenty-first-century logics of self-care, Minnie counsels Dido: "I think you get too worked up over small stuff. Stop being so sensitive and caring so much about other people and what they think about you or you gonna catch yourself a stroke, for real. You can't be bringing your work home with you" (2015: 68). The idea of enslavement as labor situates slavery within the history of capitalism. As Fred Moten describes in *In the Break*, Marx does not consider the implications of slavery for his theory of commodities or for the reality of "commodities who spoke" (2003: 36). Moten goes on to explain, "laborers who were commodities before, as it were, the abstraction of labor power from their bodies and who continue to pass on this material heritage across the divide that separates slavery and 'freedom'" (2003: 36). Understanding the history of the laboring Black body connects the work of the actors in the play with that of their characters and their characters' historical counterparts.

An Octoroon maps both the continuity and interruptions in disciplinary structures that informed the presentation of the body from the medieval period to the age of empire. For example, in the medieval and Renaissance periods, bloodlines established one's place in the social order and one's proximity to the throne. In the nineteenth century in the Americas, bloodlines conferred racial and class hierarchies that were less stable but still largely restricted physical movement and economic possibilities. In *An Octoroon* Dora asserts the planter's commitment to the Peytons as fellow elites. She asserts, "there's not a planter round here who wouldn't loan the Peytons the money to keep their name and blood amongst us" (2015: 29). Racial distinctions and social groups within races marked the individual's ability to appear as worthy of aid or disregard.

Recalling the history of the Black family's dissemblance as a result of the slave trade, Minnie and Dido tell a story of the mistaken loss of Black child. Dido details, "Yes, girl. Apparently Mas'r was about to sell Solon and Grace's baby, but then Solon switched Rebecca's baby out for they baby at the last minute and Mas'r didn't know the difference so he just sold Rebecca's dumb-ass's baby" (2015: 31). The disposability of Rebecca's baby or Solon and Grace's baby results from their blood. The Black infant's use value stems from their de-individualization, placing slavery's logic in direct contradiction to those at the heart of Enlightenment notions of the human.

An Octoroon rehearses the scene from the original play in which Zoe explains to George that she cannot wed him because she has Black blood, but, before the play arrives at Zoe's legal disqualification from civil rights (as happens in Boucicault's original), Minnie and Dido complicate the position of the enslaved not having any legal rights. Accessing their desire for George as the new master of the plantation, Minnie asks, "Would you fuck him?" Dido immediately says no to which Minnie replies, "But I kind of get the feeling you don't really get a say in the matter" (2015: 21). The exchange establishes the enslaved as desiring and feeling subjects but with no access to the protections that govern consent. As a result, while Minnie may feel attracted to George, he decides all parameters for their interactions. Her body is subject to his whim and will. The play's depiction of the enslaved women calls attention to how political autonomy circulates through desire. The play suggests that the characters become enamored as much by how proximity will position them in the world of the play as by a personal investment. The play presents coupling as already an economic proposition.

An Octoroon calls forth these stubborn racial histories of appearance to comedic effect in order to destabilize how we have historically understood the racialized body. While *The Octoroon* called into question an audience's ability to decipher race based on physical appearance, Jacobs-Jenkins's adaptation examines the meaning we ascribe once we categorize an individual. The play's first stage directions read, "*I'm just going to say this right now so we can get it over with: I don't know what a real slave sounded like. And neither do you*" (2015: 19). This initial instruction situates the primary history of diasporic Black people as a construction that emerged in relationship to acts of representation. *An Octoroon* works on that history, and in so doing, shapes the materialization of the bodies on stage.

The play not only makes a claim for how slaves sounded by deploying anachronistic language, it also challenges assumptions about the physical appearance of the enslaved. In *An Octoroon*, in order to recoup some of the debt that results from mortgages on the Terrebone Plantation, the family holds an auction. During the auction scene, the enslaved perform different roles to try and manipulate the outcome of the sale. The stage directions indicate, *"Pete, Grace, Minnie, and Dido all shuffle in awkwardly. Pete is grinning along and wearing shackles for no real reason. Minnie and Dido are wearing remarkably sexier and more revealing slave tunics and have their hair and makeup done up accordingly"* (2015: 51). The presentation of enslaved women using seduction as a mechanism to curry favor complicates the historical representation of slavery as a totalizing system of domination that evacuates any ability for the enslaved to express will. While it's important not to lose sight of the consuming and ever-present violence of slavery, representing the enslaved as desiring subjects poses a challenge to Enlightenment thought because it foregrounds the outlawed, unspeakable, fugitive movements that exist in excess of the legal and the historical (see the introduction to Fred Moten's *In the Break*).

Additionally, *An Octoroon* puts pressure on the representational field of racialized violence and the objectification of the Black body by updating what the camera captures in the play. As you will recall in *The Octoroon*, M'Closky's fiendish plot unravels when the planters see a photograph of him killing Paul and stealing the letter that would save the Terrebone Plantation from sale. The use of new technology in Boucicault's work elevated the scene and added to melodrama's signature sensationalism. In *An Octoroon* BJJ says of the use of new technology as theatrical device, "And that's basically impossible for us to do now. If anything, the theatre is no longer a place of novelty. The fact is we can more or less experience anything nowadays. So I think the final frontier, awkwardly enough, is probably just an actual experience of finality, I think" (2015: 60). This moment of reflection draws attention to what we understand as the phenomenological dimensions of theater and how interactions onstage produce an experience within the space of the theater that transforms how audience members see their own bodies and those of the actors on stage. Phenomenology focuses on how experience effects individual consciousness and although it may account for sensory qualities, it is not limited to them. In *An Octoroon*, BJJ challenges what he qualifies as the oversaturation of experience by making use of a dated technology: "*Assistant has wheeled out an overhead projector. He projects a lynching photograph onto the back wall*" (2015: 60). The use of the image calls forth the consuming and ever-present violence of the afterlives of slavery in order to expand the temporality of experience. Just as certain histories empty out the force of experience, certain ones fill it with meaning. *An Octoroon* suggests that the theater has the power to cut through the malaise of the everyday and call forth intentional relations, actions, and ways of being in the world through the materialization of bodies on stage. Through the use of the photography, *An Octoroon* demonstrates that making bodies material involves a live process rooted in deep histories that when brought to the forefront can change how we understand the body.

Within the timeframe of *An Octoroon*, Jacobs-Jenkins toggles between the present expression of Black vernacular to an iconic representation of racialized violence to raise concern about how Blackness comes to mean excess and disposability for the seemingly freer subjects of the adaptation, including BJJ. The use of Br'er Rabbit, a trickster figure found in nineteenth-century southern American folk stories and known for challenging social norms, as a character in the play signals the unfinished business of abolition skirting along the edges of Boucicault's work. The nineteenth-century playwright did not want to alienate white US viewers through his play, so he opted instead to sacrifice Zoe. *An Octoroon* calls attention to Black actors' ability to play new roles within the given structures that continue to haunt and enframe race.

Case Study: Branden Jacob-Jenkins's *Everybody*

Everybody offers a humorous rethinking of the medieval drama *Everyman* that calls into question theories of the body from the Enlightenment period to the contemporary by disrupting the desire that the actor blend seamlessly into a role. *Everybody*, like its early English antecedent, presents characters allegorically, but calls attention to the physical bodies of the actors in order to alienate viewers from them and challenges the conventional relationship between physical appearance and identity.

The play, similar to the original, depicts a character in pursuit of redemption. In this case, however, the play destabilizes the presumed masculinity of the central figure and the gender and race of all the characters. Jacob-Jenkins also updates some of the characters, for example, changing "Goods" to "Stuff." Suggesting every physical body can play each role, the play opens with a lottery. The stage directions state, "Usher reenters, interrupting. Usher in a coat, keys in hand, and carries a portable bingo cage or a similar lottery device" (2020: 19). The Usher states:

> So, you may or may not already know this from the marketing materials but, in this play, it is specified that the actors' roles from this point forward be decided by lottery every night. This is done in an attempt to more closely thematize the randomness of death while also destabilizing your preconceived notions about identity, et cetera, et cetera, blah, blah, blah. Honestly, all it really means is that our incredible ensemble of performers here has memorized the entire script but have just received—or are receiving—one of five roles to play tonight and, in all likelihood, you are about to see a version of the show which has never been performed out of 120 possible variations. (2020: 19)

The dismissive "blah, blah, blah" marks the post-structuralist notion of identity as a social construction as perhaps passé. Nevertheless, through the specific ways the play challenges the hierarchy of mind over body, it explicates the power dynamics at the heart of the body's appearance for its audience and calls for a rethinking of the histories that shape contemporary understandings of the body.

Before assigning roles, the Usher, who also speaks as God, offers a brief history that challenges the hierarchies of mind and spirit over body as instantiated in Christian theology and reconfigured in the age of empire and beyond through the designation of certain populations as thinking subjects and other ones as property. The stage direction indicates, "'God,' who is unseen, speaks through the Usher. 'God's' voice is non-human" (2020: 10). The stage directions continue, "God speaks through the Usher (reduced now to a physical vessel for God's words)"; he says:

BECAUSE OF THE VESSEL I HAVE CHOSEN? / BECAUSE I HAVE NO EYES? / WHAT NEED WOULD I HAVE FOR THESE PUNY ORGANS? / TO APPREHEND THIS MINOR PLANE OF MATTER / AND ILLUSION / THAT I'VE LET YOU INHABIT? / I. WHO HAVE USHERED EVERY DETAIL OF THIS WORLD / INTO BEING– / AND MOVE IT FORWARD WITH MY VERY BREATH, / WHICH IS TIME? (2020: 11)

The use of ventriloquism (God speaking through the Usher's body) establishes that the transcendent has no use for puny human organs but must make use of them to communicate in this context. The body, therefore, has use value but no intrinsic value. It functions as a tool to deliver information but is not a source of information. The play also, however, opens the door for the takeover of any body via its unorthodox casting. While historically certain bodies have held the distinction of disposability or being primarily for use (such as Zoe in *The Octoroon*), in *Everybody*, the history of racial, gender, and class exploitation of bodies is destabilized. In so doing, the play ironically affirms the value of historically exploited bodies by calling attention to the hierarchies of mind and body that have historically enabled such discriminatory practices in general.

In anticipation of the accounting that Everybody will make before God, the player tries to convince people and ideas to come along for the journey. In an effort to induce Stuff's participation, Everybody laments "my labor has been literally translated into the abstract value with which I purchased you, so in some ways you are actually the sum total of how I spent a lot of my time on this planet; so I'm begging you, go with me and keep me company and help me support my presentation" (2020: 37). The assertion offers a Marxist reading of labor as the materialization of bodily exertion in the formation or procurement of property—in this case, stuff. As Marx explains in *Capital*, we access labor products "through the relations which the act of exchange establishes between products" (1990: 165). The animation of products, or "Stuff," as a character once again shifts presumed hierarchies, here between people and objects as stuff appears as a "thing" through its ability (distinct from an object) to "[demand] that people confront it on its own terms; thus, a thing forces a person into an awareness of the self in material relation to the thing" (Bernstein 2009: 69–70). Stuff calls attention to the physical exertion Everybody expresses as an expression of accumulation that offers a different entry point into how we understand identity. In this example, the play suggests that the relay between subject and thing offers as much insight into Everybody as a summary judgment by the viewer or by God.

While, for the most part, people are understood to have dominion over objects, performance theorists such as Fred Moten have contemplated how the history of slavery, turning human beings into property, challenges Marx's depiction of labor and its theoretical divide between human and object. In *Everybody*, as in Moten's critique, the commodity shows resistance and, in so doing, destabilizes its pure use value. At the beginning of their interaction, Stuff assures Everybody, "I am here to help you with any problem in the world. How much do you need?" (2020: 37). After Everybody makes the request, Stuff first tries to avoid participation, pointing out the difficulty often associated with moving objects, particularly given a penchant for accumulation, and then realizing Everybody will not be deterred, he has to disabuse the titular figure of misconceptions about ownership. Stuff explains,

I guess I'm just so enchanting or comforting or beautiful or there's some sort of Object Relational Thing in your programming that I exploit or something but, at the end of the day, I just ... ruin you. I've done it again and again and I'm sorry. Because, honestly, what's going to happen is that, when you're dead, some other helpless Somebody is just going to come along and I'm just going to wind up doing the same cruel thing to them. (2020: 38)

Stuff places itself in a repetitive relationship to Everybody rather than in a subordinate position. The idea of accumulation as a result of the laboring body shifts when commodities speak from a hierarchy to engagement.

The philosophical shift that Foucault describes facilitated the understanding of individual will that had emerged in relationship to the Enlightenment and accompanied the disciplining of the body toward use and efficiency. Jacobs-Jenkins's *Everybody* calls that shift into humorous relief through presenting a protagonist losing control of the body. Near the end of *Everybody*, Love has a conversation with the titular protagonist about their body and how physical deterioration with age causes a crisis of control. Once Everybody echoes disdain for change and lack of control they agree, "I DON'T LOVE– ... THAT I HAVE NO CONTROL" (2020: 45). By the end of the scene, Everybody concedes, "BUT I HAVE NO CONTROL! ... THIS BODY IS JUST MEAT! ... I SURRENDER! ... I HAVE NO CONTROL" (2020: 45). The last lines of the scene affirm how the individual's autonomy correlates to control over the body, but *Everybody* challenges the idea of control as an expression of power and instead establishes the body's ability to exert it's force.

Scene XIII consists of stage directions that read "*Skeletons dance macabre in a landscape of pure light and sound*" (2020: 46). Instead of reasserting the subordination of the body, subjects become interchangeable and skeletons dance on their own in the play. Drawing the audience into understanding the body's epistemological work and ability to negotiate the structures of power that Foucault describes, the next scene features Love and Everybody both naked. Animating the surveillance at the heart of theater spectatorship, their disrobing directs the audience's gaze. Unlike the economic implications of surveillance "as an internal part of the production machinery and as a specific mechanism in the disciplinary power" (Foucault 1995: 175), the work of directing the gaze in this case serves to establish the body as source of information and not just the object of spectatorial consumption. The presentation of the undisciplined, dying body asserts the physical claims that can be made on the person and the ways bodies speak back.

Everybody leverages the tension between understandings of the body in the medieval period and the contemporary one to humorous effect. Similar to an early moment in the play of ventriloquism as Everybody continues the journey, the stage directions read: "*Lights rise slowly on Everybody, who is now listening to two Somebodies speak in unison, but it is somehow Everybody's voice coming out of both of their mouths: a double lip-synch*" (2020: 28). The use of voice-over calls attention to the specific bodily properties as circulating and not the unique possession of the individual. In the play, the moment of dispossession calls attention to the associations Everybody takes for granted. The scene features a discussion among the Somebodies but with Everybody's voice of the difference between friendship and kinship. Everybody reasons:

The very basis of your Self is just a genetic mishmash of other Selves. You are a part of something. Think of the long line of accidents and miracles and struggles and victories that it took to bring you into life. When you hold all that in your head, doesn't it almost feel like … like … sacred or holy or—that the very fact of your being alive proves a connection between you and the very beginning of everything, to—to "God." And that connection is your family. Wait! Your family may actually help here! Kinship is way different than friendship! You share the same biological information, so that means they're genetically programmed to be immediately sympathetic, because whatever happens to you is sort of happening to them, too. And some of your family members have known you since before you were even aware of yourself as a Self, so they could also help you with this presentation of how you've lived your life and why—Where is your family? Maybe one of them will come with you! Find your family! (2020: 29)

Everybody learns from the moment of disembodiment that they should double down on connection being in the blood, a comment on how desire functions in opposition to material realities. The play offers a comedic rendering of the ongoing investment in biological notions of the body and the connections it produces as genetic rather than social. The idea of sharing the same biological information produces expectations for connection that are rarely met and, nevertheless, often understood as the ideal mode of social organization. The play pokes fun at Everybody's reasoning having his voice, presumably his unique physiological property, coming out of the mouths of Friendship and Kinship. If physical traits transfer along genetic lines, then Friendship should not be able to adopt Everybody's voice. In the play, however, who belongs to what role, familial or otherwise, varies.

Everybody destabilizes the appearance of the body as a manifestation of kinship, gender, and race. Theories of race and gender as performance account for how history and power have rendered identity fixed rather than a set of embodied and rhetorical practices repeated over time. In "Performative Acts and Gender Constitution," Butler argues:

> gender is instated through acts which are internally discontinuous, then the *appearance of substance* is precisely that, a constructed identity, a performative accomplishment which the mundane social audience, including the actors themselves, come to believe and to perform in the mode of belief. (1990: 154)

The accumulative effect of gender through a series of constituted acts functions in specific ways depending on how the performance intersects with the race and class of the audience and actors. While gender has in some quarters become loosened from the body, particularly given the distinction between gender and sex, race still remains closely tied to physical characteristics, primarily skin tone and hair texture.

Jacobs-Jenkins's adaptations comment on how the theater has historically grappled with representing the body on stage. His plays provide commentary on early works to question what historical and social shifts enable understanding the materialization of the body on stage. How does the body transform from a fixed form of evidence to an active participant in making meaning on stage? What does the body teach us about how history, power, culture, religion, and social context work together to materialize meaning?

In Section 2, I consider three case studies to examine how, in the wake of the Second World War, theorists grappled with questions about the relationship between human action and identity and how the development of new theories of embodied action helped to constitute the individual. I ask what histories, power dynamics, circumstances, and relationships give repeated actions constitutive force?

SECTION TWO

Extended Case Studies

Introduction

This section will focus on three case studies: Jean Genet's *The Balcony* (1957), Tony Kushner's *Angels in America* (Parts 1 and 2) (1991), and Suzan-Lori Parks's *Father Comes Home from the Wars* (Parts 1, 2, and 3) (2015) that are each set in specific historical turning points (respectively the Second World War, the AIDS epidemic, and the American Civil War), which influence perceptions of the body through changes in labor, medical, and social practices. The three plays each consider how illusion, rhetoric, space, and time shape the appearance of the body. These devices deployed in the plays raise larger questions about the use of the body as visual evidence and a source for truth claims. As outlined in the previous section, performances offer the physical body of actors as evidence even as they question the audience's perceptions of the actors and the characters that the actors play. What does the appearance of the body teach us about how history, power, culture, religion, and social context materialize the body? Individually, the playwrights of my case study texts develop specific styles and techniques that call attention to how bodies emerge in space and time and through presumptions about identity categories. In addition, *Angels in America* and *Father Comes Home from the Wars* call into question what bodies we associate with the philosophical category of the human. As discussed in Section 1 in Western philosophy, from Descartes to Marx, ideas about the body and its relationship to the mind or its deployment in labor presume a white male body. In response to these assumptions, Judith Butler describes how the materiality of the body, its physical presence in the world, reflects a set of historical practices and desires for gender. Fred Moten explains how Black people's experiences disrupt Marx's theory of the laboring body producing commodities by accounting for the experiences of the enslaved, people that were commodities. How does the materialization of the body differ when the human is defined through histories that account for normative and nonnormative bodies?

These writers offer representations of the body that draw on theoretical shifts after the Second World War. Nazi Germany's genocide in the Holocaust and the United States' use of nuclear weapons on Hiroshima and Nagasaki shift conceptions about a government's ability and willingness to enact mass death. In the aftermath of the war, theorists began to reexplore the meaning of life and the impact of human action on society. Reflecting on the impact of a world-shifting war, theorists began to grapple with the existential crisis of mass precarity, millions of people in poverty, and widespread food insecurity. In 1946, the United Nations founded the Food and Agricultural Organization to address uneven access to and supply of food.

In post-Second World War theater, the general emphasis on individual agency, or lack thereof, calls attention to a sense of hopelessness in the face of possible world annihilation. The drama foregrounds the relationship between an individual's actions and the structures (political, economic, social) that govern their lives, but artists disagree about the nature of that relationship. Some artists believed that individuals could reform structures to better attend to the needs of the people. Conversely, Genet's The Balcony suggests people have limited capacities to alter their specific conditions or history more generally. Decades later, Kushner's Angels in America depicts characters mounting radical rearrangements of the historical order. The Balcony maps the individual's limitations through a persistent presentation of the body in pain while Angels in

America depicts the diseased and institutionalized body as a site of possibility. Parks's *Father Comes Home from the Wars* (Parts 1, 2, and 3) affirms the individual's ability to change his or her circumstances but only through covert projects that remain largely imperceptible within the systems that organize society.

As discussed in Section 1, Michel Foucault questioned the relationship between power and knowledge and he suggested rethinking how institutions (hospitals, schools, prisons) function, which challenges the idea of unilateral power to control the habits of behaviors. Foucault suggested that individual actors, through the expression of their bodies, constantly exchange power with institutions, usually by ceding their authority. His theories are useful in examining the body in pain, particularly since punishment has been a persistent scene of enactment from medieval to modern theater. In *Discipline and Punish: The Birth of the Prison*, Foucault theorizes the interdependence of public violence and community consolidation. He asserts, "The public execution did not re-establish justice; it reactivated power" (1995: 49) and contends that public displays of violence discipline the body and serve a reciprocal purpose; they establish the role of the discipliner as those displays subordinate the disciplined. In this case, the executioner may seem to hold complete power over the body, but Foucault contends that if that were so, he would not need to repeatedly assert his power. Through the act of execution the state consolidates power that actually flows among citizens and governmental officials. The executioner himself, however, does not hold the power but instead represents the disciplinary apparatus that is the state. Foucault makes clear that part of what maintains power is the misperception that institutions sustain their dominance without human action.

Like Foucault's writing about power, *Angels in America* and *Father Comes Home from the Wars* both express similar post-structuralist notions of the permeability of power relations. In *Angels in America*, as I will discuss in this section, the porous body serves as a metaphor for the permeability of other borders: political, social, familial, national, and social. Similarly,

Father Comes Home from the Wars depicts the body of the enslaved to challenge the Enlightenment idea of subjectivity as universally accessible to all humans. In addition, *Father Comes Home* suggests that individuals who the state does not recognize as subjects may operate in alternative socialites: underground and off-grid, challenging the comprehensiveness of overarching systems such as slavery.

The Balcony illustrates the horrors of war and the precarious position of women's bodies in the midst of social upheaval. Whether within the brothel or in the city, women's bodies functioned in service of men. As the plays of Kushner and Parks suggest, cross-cutting histories of race, gender, and sexuality informed how individuals intervene in reshaping historical, discursive, and social attachments to normative presentations of the body. The plays of Kushner and Parks press against the limit of the individual's relationship to, dependence on, and subjection to others. All three case studies draw attention to how the body serves as a site to understand social and historical contexts as well as psychic and economic systems.

Case Study 1: Jean Genet's *The Balcony*

Jean Genet's *The Balcony*, first published in French in 1956 and first performed in English in London at the Arts Theatre Club in 1957, depicts the cyclical and, therefore, perhaps futile nature of political revolt. The play opens in a brothel that distinguishes itself by operating as a house of mirrors. As the madam of the brothel, Irma, describes, "The Grand Balcony has a world-wide reputation. It's the most artful, yet the most decent house of illusions" (1966: 34). Genet's drama stages a battle over which political allegory will organize society: the full and unimpeachable power of a sovereign or the shared power of individuals through democracy. Throughout the play, the Grand Balcony remains at the heart of the battle, a site where patrons and workers produce fantasies more seductive than the participants' lived realities. The setting calls attention to the disposability of and disregard for women's bodies, suggesting they have limited access to either political allegory and, instead, function to support them. As with any performing art, the body shows up in both predictable and surprising ways, blurring the line between the real and the fake, actual existence, and appearance.

Genet's play intervenes in an enduring conversation about the relationship between the real and the fake, harkening back to Plato's "Allegory of the Cave," which depicts people that have been imprisoned in an underground cavern since childhood. The prisoners chains prevent them from moving freely and, as a result, they are only able to see shadows cast upon the wall in front of them rather than the people or objects that produce the shadows. Due to the prisoner's limited perspective, the shadows encompass reality, which differs from those casting the shadows. Nevertheless, an individual's position limits his or her perceptions because it informs how the body makes sense of the world. Within the particular context of a new mid-century theatrical genre, the theater of the absurd still evidences some of the central concerns Plato expressed, calling attention to the limits of individual perception and agency. Martin Esslin explains:

> The Theatre of the Absurd … can be seen as the reflection of what seems to be the attitude most genuinely representative of our own time. The hallmark of this attitude is its sense that the certitudes and unshakable basic assumptions of former ages have been swept away, that they have been tested and found wanting, that they have been discredited as cheap and somewhat childish illusions. The decline of religious faith was masked until the end of the Second World War by the substitute religions of faith in progress, nationalism, and various totalitarian fallacies. All this was shattered by the war. (1996: 31)

The Theatre of the Absurd calls attention to the seeming mutual benefit of an individual abdicating his or her power to institutions or systems that seem to order reality and give purpose to reality. Esslin explains that these systems: "progress, nationalism, and various totalitarian fallacies" proved empty following the Second World War.

Genet's version of theater of the absurd intersects with Esslin's description and also recalls Antonin Artaud's Theatre of Cruelty, a form of avant-garde theater developed in the 1930s that focused on communion between the actor and audience, intended to shock the audience. Artaud concretized his thinking in *The Theatre and Its Double* (1938). Genet's drama shares with Artaud an interest in considering the impact of violence and its theatrical reenactment on stage. While violence injures the individual, that experience does not have wider impact. Therefore, changes in individual perception and experience occur but do not have a wider impact on the surrounding dynamics. *The Balcony* maintains that any human action, staged or otherwise, does not have the power to change collectives of people, social situations, or political outcomes.

Power Play: Revealing the Impact of Individual's Perception

The Balcony opens in the midst of a scene reminiscent of both *Everyman* and *Everybody* as it foregrounds the theoretical ties between conceptions of the body in religious and theatrical spaces. The play draws attention to how rituals associated with religious rites translate to not only theatrical presentations of the body but also what the body comes to represent in intimate spaces. The play opens in a carefully described room: "On the ceiling, a chandelier, which will remain the same in each scene. The set seems to represent a sacristy, formed by three blood-red, cloth folding-screens. The one at the rear has a built-in door. Above, a huge Spanish crucifix, drawn in trompe l'oeil" (1966: 7). Three people occupy the space, a man dressed as a Bishop sitting in a chair, a young woman drying her hands on a towel and a third woman, Irma. The use of stage props and costumes situate the audience within the context of a religious ritual. There is a Spanish crucifix drawn to appear three dimensionally (trompe l'oeil) and a man dressed as a religious figure (a bishop). The play invites certain associations, but what other truths organize this scene besides the ones that are readily apparent? A deconstructive mode of analysis might begin to consider how power informs the appearance of truth, emphasizing that many truths may exist and that a singular truth does not reside with a religious figure or a king. The opening scene seems to suggest the man dressed as the bishop holds the power, following Foucault's idea that disciplinary systems produce the subjugated bodies. In *Discipline and Punish*, Foucault traces the development of disciplinary systems to the eighteenth century and explains, "The historical moment of the disciplines was the moment when an art of the human body was born, which was directed not only at the growth of its skills, nor at intensification of its subjection, but at the formation of a relation that in the mechanism itself makes it more obedient as it becomes more useful, and conversely" (1995: 137–8). His genealogy calls attention to the societal structures that produce relationships between the individual body, i.e., the laboring body, and a structure, i.e., capitalism. How does the man introduced at the top of the action come to power and what devices (costumes, props, and scenic design) supplement it?

Penance organizes the opening of Genet's play and places the body and its adornments center stage. The stage directions indicate:

> The Bishop, in mitre and gilded cope, is sitting in the chair. He is obviously larger than life. The role is played by an actor wearing tragedian's cothurni [boots] about twenty inches high. His shoulders, on which the cope lies are inordinately broadened so that when the curtain rises he looks huge and stiff, like a scarecrow. He wears garish make-up. (1966: 7)

Producing a physically imposing presence, the Bishop's boots add significantly to his height, making the average-size man appear a towering figure. In addition, the padding on his shoulders makes his width as unbelievable as his height, so much so that the Bishop first appears to be more of a mannequin used to scare away animals than a human animal himself. The costuming suggests that the audience has entered into a ritualistic drama driven by this imposing figure. The play, however, invites a rethinking of the power that this figure holds by describing him as more of a mannequin than a monarch.

Recall, three people occupy the space, a man dressed as a Bishop sitting in a chair, a young woman drying her hands on a towel, and a second woman, Irma. The presentation of the Bishop blurs the line between how theater participates in a practice of "make believe" rather than what performance theorist Richard Schechner calls "make belief" (2002: 35). Schechner's distinction suggests theater functions primarily on a narrative rather ideological level, transforming narratives rather belief systems. Instead of suggesting a clean break between ideas, belief systems, and the world of the imagination, theater, Schechner draws attention to how theater participates in philosophy. In his most well-known book, *Between Theatre and Anthropology* (1985), Schechner questions the distinctions between understanding theater as what happens on proscenium-arch-framed stages and acting that occurs in other places. Particularly since conventions of theater differ around the world (from stages, to immersive theater, to happenings in galleries), he advocates for a capacious term to describe aesthetic modes of embodiment—performance. For Schechner, performance is "'showing' dong ... pointing to, underlining, and displaying doing" (2002: 22). The blurring of the line between what happens on a stage and everyday acts also enables a closer understanding of how theater relates to theoretical conversations about the world more generally. As the opening scene of *The Balcony* suggests, what we understand as dramatic action and the everyday performance of erotic role play may blend into one another. Based on the position of the audience member, it may be difficult to tell one from the other.

The Balcony draws attention to how bodies in motion put pressure on the boundaries between redemptive and condemned behaviors, suggesting ethical standards shift given the context of the act. The Bishop details how the woman should seek repentance for her purported sins, saying "I saw there the greedy longing for transgression. In flooding it, evil all at once baptized it. Her big eyes opened on the abyss ... a deathly pallor lit up—yes, Madame—lit up her face. But our holiness lies only in our being able to forgive you your sins" (1966: 10). Nevertheless, he concedes, "Even if they're only make-believe" (1966: 10). Revealing based on his concession, the man plays the role of Bishop not just as any actor playing a role in a theatrical production but within the play, *The Balcony* features a performance within the performance as the woman asks, "And what if my sins were real" (1966: 10)? Rebuffed he responds (as the stage direction indicates, "in a different, less theatrical tone"), "You're mad! I hope you really didn't do all that!" (1966: 10). The exchange between the penitent and the Bishop calls attention to how embodied acts have different implications based on the contexts and belief systems that underpin them. Does the ritual of absolution lose its force outside of the Christian church and does "sinful" behavior cease to violate moral codes when it occurs under the guise of make believe? Theories of power and history help explain how ritualized acts, such as religious rites, continue to produce social relationships even when those acts are removed from the usual context of a church to a theater.

The opening scene also calls attention to how the physical body appears on stage as a function of historical beliefs and contemporary contexts. The presentation of the Bishop "in mitre and gilded cope" establishes that in the world of the play he will function as a religious figure. As we learn, simply donning certain attire does not transform the individual into the role but it does offer onlookers a set of visual cues that situate the person in a history of ideas. The costume helps to satisfy the desire for the character in the play to act as a Bishop as does the practice of offering absolution for sins that have only happened in the actors' imaginations. The play within the play draws attention to the material conditions that situate individuals in their social roles.

The third scene of *The Balcony* also features a performance that shapes the appearance of the body but this case requires a more strenuous act of "make belief." Here a man acting as the General commands a girl to act as his horse. He instructs: "All right, but first, down on your knees! Come on, come on, bend your knees, bend them ... (*The Girl rears, utters a whinny of pleasure and kneels like a circus horse before the General*)" (1966: 23). Although the Girl does not appear to actually be a horse, her ability to approximate the sound and movements of the animal draws attention to the distinction between humans and others, and the idea of being in physical service to another. Although the women in the play function for and at the pleasure of their male clients, they also exert control through their willingness or unwillingness to abide by the script. The third scene ends with the General rehearsing his untimely death as the woman-turned-horse drags him in a carriage. He plays dead, which will filter from the play-within-the-play to the play itself and draw attention to a permeable border between make believe and make belief. The happenings of the brothel are for fun, are acts of make-believe, but *The Balcony* suggests they have just as little and as much impact on the world outside as they do on the inner workings of the house.

The play establishes that the line between ideological and artistic narratives may be less finely demarcated than it appears. As such, art has great power in its ability to craft narratives that reinforce beliefs but, as this play will conclude, little impact on changing belief systems. By the end of the play, the Grand Balcony remains in place as other societal structures crumble. As an embodied form, theater draws attention to how actions have limited impact on the perceptions of bodies. While theater specializes in the transformation of bodies before the eyes of spectators, the play suggests that the historical and ideological investments of viewers remain intact and attached to the body even as we witness these transformations. Theater then must not only intercede in what we see but also comment on how we come to see.

Marxism and Post-Marxism: Materialism and Power

As the play unfolds, we learn that each scene includes an intricate set design that produces the appearance of the scenario. The design envelops patrons into the world of the Grand Balcony, the brothel that houses the central action of the play. These material structures produce familiarity through historical, social, and cultural cues, just as the bodies on stage—their adornment, positions, and speech acts—tap into customs that situate them in place and time. Scenes toggle back and forth between physical reality and staged reality, from the opening with the Bishop pretending to offer absolution to the reality that he participates in a sex game, drawing attention to a central question in theater and performance studies: how does one distinguish between the real and the fake?

The setting of the play in a city undergoing a revolution that contains a brothel also draws attention to how the body participates in economic systems and particular forms of gender-specific labor. This recalls Marx's attention to how economic systems, particularly capitalism, have a totalizing logic that organizes society. Marxism does not account for the devaluation of women's labor. Meaning, within a capitalist system, women's labor has less value than the labor of men. The disparity is not fundamental to capitalism per se but a function of social hierarchies that become embedded within the capitalist system. Therefore, when analyzing the body from a Marxist perspective that focuses on value and labor, one must account for how social and historical views of that labor in terms of race and gender overlap with economic evaluations. In the Western world, the constitution of the other has distorted economic and psychic arrangements.

Genet's play invites a post-Marxist analysis, one that deconstructs Marx's views, because it focuses on the labor of women. In traditional Marxism, class differences produced by economic structures are the primary form of difference. A post-Marxist interpretation considers how economic structures function in relationship to gendered social norms. A brothel, then, calls attention to how women's roles in society determine their economic power and not their inherent value as laborers. A patriarchal understanding of women as sexual objects underpins the logics of a brothel. Throughout the play, the violence erupting in the city spills into the Grand Balcony as does the "consensual" violence within the rooms of the brothel.

In the opening scene, as the Bishop tries to deduce if his scene partner, the young woman, has actually committed the sins at the heart of their role play, the stage directions indicate that from another room, "The same terrible scream is heard again" (1966: 10). While the expression of pain, just like penance, could be an act, the anguish disrupts the scripted behavior and pulls the participants from their rehearsal back to their reality. The scream calls attention to the potential for physical injury even within the context of a scripted performance. The material conditions require the performer to risk her body as a part of the production. While *The Balcony* scripts the potential for physical risk within sex work, it also exists as a backdrop to live performance in general. Situating the world of the play along a spectrum other than ritual, it also calls attention to how theater approximates intimate forms of labor. In *The Balcony*, however, the breaks usher in the metatheatrical commentary as they call attention to the quotidian nature of performance and gendered violence.

In another case of judgment that echoes the disciplinary apparatus that enables the body to appear, Scene 2 depicts a Thief pleading with a Judge for clemency. The proceeding interlaces subjection to the law and economic systems with ritualized performance. As Foucault explains, "If economic exploitation separates the force and the product of labour, let us say that disciplinary coercion establishes in the body the constricting link between an increased aptitude and an increased domination" (1995: 138). Capitalism separates the work of making a coat from the product purchased in the store. Foucault suggests, regimes of discipline induce the Thief's ability to play a role that results in her violation; the more effective she is in her performance, the greater her exploitation. However, as the Executioner, the third member of the scenario, explains, the confession must be induced. Responding to the too-soon confession, the Executioner reminds the Thief, "That's for later ... I mean the confession is supposed to come later. Plead not guilty." Bemused, the Thief responds, "What, and get beaten again!" (1966: 15). Although the brothel employs the Executioner, he has no allegiance to the Thief. He serves the needs of the client. The Judge explains, "Exactly, my child: and get beaten. You must first deny, then admit and repent. I want to see hot tears gush from your lovely eyes. Oh! I want you to be drenched in them. The power of tears!" (1966: 15). The negotiation among participants continues throughout the scene which produces some question about whether the Executioner actually hurts the Thief or if he just pretends to do so. The "backstage" conversation among the brothel workers suggests that he does mete out punishment, reinforcing the blurred distinction between theatrical and quotidian performance. The implied sexual acts that distinguish The Balcony also blur the line. As a result, the actor's labor becomes akin to other forms of subjection.

Although *The Balcony* focuses on the ideological impact of revolt, it also calls attention to physical and material impact in terms of how individuals must labor and the conditions for that work. Subsequently, the Executioner (also known as Arthur) and Irma discuss the material costs of his actions. Arthur asserts, "The banker wants to see stripes on her back. So I stripe it" (1966: 43). Irma, pointing to the prurient interests of the patron and, perhaps, those of *The Balcony*'s audience, charges, "At least you don't get any pleasure out of it?" To which he responds, "Not with her. You're my only love. And a job's a job. I'm conscientious about my work" (1966: 43). The exchange renders the body of the Girl in service to others. While Arthur also presents himself as labor, his proximity to Irma mitigates, although does not eliminate, his risk of injury. Irma clarifies pragmatically, "I'm not jealous of the girl, but I wouldn't want you to disable the personnel. It's getting harder and harder to replace" (1966: 43). Arthur's response establishes the physical requirements of performing even in the absence of scripted danger. He explains,

> I tried a couple of times to draw marks on her back with purple paint, but it didn't work. The old guy inspects her when he arrives and insists I deliver her in good shape. ... (*shrugging his shoulders*). What's one illusion more or less! I thought I was doing the right thing. But don't worry. Now I whip, I flagellate, she screams, and he crawls. (1966: 43)

The physical exertion in reenactment changes the body and situates it on a continuum with ritual performance that expects a physical change to evidence a spiritual one. Even in Genet's modern drama, the body remains a site to work through social and ethical demands.

The Balcony demonstrates how the repeated actions of performers and the setting for their actions contribute to interpretations of the body. Just as the physical acts shape the body, either through violence or work, so do they inform the appearance of the body for the audience. Irma's assistant, Carmen, calls attention to the relationship between roles and appearance. She questions Irma,

> When our sessions are over, Madame, you never allow anyone to talk about them. So you have no idea of how we really feel. You observe it all from a distance. But if ever you once put on the dress and the blue veil, or if you were the

unbuttoned penitent, or the general's mare, or the country girl tumbled in the hay. (1966: 30)

Carmen's critique reveals the surveillance that structures the Grand Balcony.

For the workers, the brothel mimics the structure of the theater as a place that invites looking and produces furtive glances. The Grand Balcony structures looking by calling attention to the ever-presence of the gaze without locating it specifically, which encourages the sex workers to perform for their clients and Irma as well. As such, the Grand Balcony functions in ways similar to Foucault's description of the panopticon—a system of disciplinary power deployed in eighteenth-century prisons but that also applies to other institutions.

The Grand Balcony also allows sounds from outside the city and between rooms to bleed into one another; the structure calls attention to its insecurity. In so doing, the sound heightens the anxiety of the patrons, encouraging them to stay long enough to complete their scenarios but not too long thereafter. As the tensions of revolt escalate in the city, Irma reflects that the Chief of Police, George, will not arrive in time to protect her establishment. She says,

They'll succeed in surrounding the house before George arrives. ... One thing we mustn't forget—if ever we get out of this mess—is that the walls aren't sufficiently padded and the windows aren't well sealed. ... One can hear all that's going on in the street. Which means that from the street one can hear what's going on in the house. (1966: 34)

The spilling in and out of action from the street to the brothel and back again informs the unfolding of events in both places. It also adds to the dynamic of having something hidden in plain sight or the suggestion that their activities are supposed to be separate from the revolt in the city but, according to the logics of the play, actually deeply participate in their unfolding.

The apparatus of visual control, the house of mirrors, cannot protect against the unfolding of violence within and outside of the brothel. The violence structures both places and situates them in relationship to one another. The violence that occurs within the brothel calls attention to the value that women's bodies have in exchange but also to the lack of protection that they experience within patriarchy. The limited power that the women of the Grand Balcony claim draws attention to how bodies function in a labor economy that is also subject to a gender hierarchy. The combination enables both the women to sustain themselves and for the play to reveal the belief systems that limit the women's power. Although theatrical display differs from surveillance, the power structures that adhere in both cases of looking function through their ability to assess from a distance. At the same time, Carmen suggests that the act of participating in the scenes produces attachments that are not readily perceivable from a distance or through observation. The impact of the performance may only be fully understood through experience, suggesting the audience both participates in the dynamic and stands at a critical distance from it.

Much of the play calls into question whether actions can actually change history. The play, ironically, suggests that human action is ineffective in making historical change as the play makes history through the daily actions of the actors and the transformation of their bodies. The laboring body and the body in pain serve as the play's central images. As Carmen details, the intimate acts with patrons transform the body as a source of knowledge, point of exchange, and an object in relation to another. She recalls how Irma watched "the bank-clerk from the National City kneeling before [her] and swooning when I appeared to him. Unfortunately, he had his back to you and so you weren't aware of the ecstasy on his face and the wild pounding of my heart. My blue veil, my blue robe, my blue apron, my blue eyes" (1966: 38). As performance theorist Amber Musser details in her book *Sensual Excess*, "Desire consolidates the subject, even as it privileges its momentary dissolve" (2018: 7). Carmen as a source of desire for the patron has a privileged perspective that accompanies her subordination. The sensual exchange complicates the relationship between Carmen and the patron and the knowledge the exchange produces as she toggles back and forth from object of desire to agent of pleasure. In addition, the positioning of the bodies precludes certain points of view. Irma is unable to see the bank-clerk's expression because Carmen's body hides it from view. Nevertheless, Irma knows her clients. When Carmen describes the client's eye color, Irma corrects, "They're hazel," but Carmen quickly responds, "They were blue that day" (1966: 38). While likely a joke, the exchange demonstrates how the body's appearance, its perception by the viewer, depends on the physical positions of actors and observers. At the same time, swooning in ecstasy likely reflects physiological changes (i.e., increased heart rate and perspiration) that coincide with excitement and pleasure.

Psychoanalysis: Appearance and Illusions

As a house that functions through mirrors that reflect the action happening in each room, *The Balcony* stages reflections of and on the erotic scenes to depict the body as an illusion, but one that has a material reality and history. Although Genet published *The Balcony* well before Jacques Lacan's *Ecrits* (1970), through the play's use of mirrors it anticipates Lacan's ideas, as described in his essay "The Mirror Stage as Formative of the *I* Function." Lacan's work, along with the writing of Sigmund Freud, is foundational for psychoanalytic theory— that structures human behavior as the interaction among the ego, the id, and the super ego, building on the writing of Freud. In the essay Lacan argues that the ego emerges through the infant's identification with what he or she sees in the mirror. He describes:

> It suffices to understand the mirror stage in this context *as an identification* in the full sense analysis gives to the term: namely, the transformation that takes place in the subject when he assumes an image—an image that is seemingly predestined to have an effect that this phase, as witnessed by the use in analytic theory of antiquity's term, "imago." (1977: 76)

In other words, one's relationship to the body emerges through one's alienation from oneself. The sense of self is introduced through an "other" in the form of an image. The I finds itself through the image which is fundamentally a moment of misrecognition.

A psychoanalytical reading of *The Balcony* would consider how the characters experience the brothel as a site of identification that produces an image that relates to the self but also reflects the desires for and alienation from the self. In the fourth scene of the play, one that consists primarily of pantomime, the stage directions indicate, "*All the gestures of the little old man are reflected in the three mirrors. (Three actors are needed to play the roles of the reflections)*" (1966: 28). The scene features an interaction between the Girl (who works at the brothel) and The Man. The Girl treats the man to a lice-infested wig that she shoves on his head and threatens him with a whip that she uses to lash flowers from his hand. The actors in the mirrors would reflect the Man, perhaps clutching his hand after the flowers have been whipped away or touching the wig to feel for infestation. The scene literalizes what Lacan depicts as a reflection. The actors replicate The Man's action, producing a form of citation and, as Amber Musser argues, "citation can alter the boundaries of the self" (2018: 4). The reflections support the idea of the body's knowledge production circulating between people and, through Musser's reading, both expands the boundaries of the individual and highlight his or her participation in the citational practice. At the same time, the sex play foregrounds the materiality of the interaction between The Girl and The Man because the Man actually risks injury.

The play calls attention to how psychoanalytic framing must account for the material conditions and histories of how bodies appear differently in the world not only in terms of gender but as gender intersects with sex, race, class, and sexuality.

The reflections on the scenes, already highlighted through Irma's comments, reemerges in her interaction with the Chief of Police who laments that he has not become a figure worthy of impersonation or being remembered via performance. He accuses Irma of thwarting his desired outcome, noting how she produces the Grand Balcony's illusions. He charges, "You've got secret peep-holes in every wall. Every partition, every mirror, is rigged. In one place, you can hear the sighs in another the echo of the moans. You don't need me to tell you that brothel tricks are mainly mirror tricks" (1966: 48). The Chief of Police discloses the inner workings of the apparatus that keeps the patrons satisfied through the production of the illusion that confirms their desire but, even in disclosure, the impact does not wholly shift as demonstrated by many of the men pausing mid-scene to question the unfolding of events or remarking on outside sounds that seep into the scene. The permeability of the brothel structure does not unravel the illusion but rather reinforces it.

Calling attention to the relationship between what unfolds in the city and the illusions the Grand Balcony propagates, The Chief of Police concludes, "But I'll make my image detach itself from me. I'll make it penetrate into your studios, force its way in, reflect and multiply itself. Irma, my function weighs me down. Here, it will appear to me in the blazing light of pleasure and death. (*Musingly*) Of death" (1966: 48). The Chief wants to be immortalized in order to facilitate his legacy as an illusion. His comment highlights the greater investment in an ideal than in the self.

At the end of their conversation, Irma reminds the Chief why Arthur works for her. Because the Chief required

> there being a man here—against my better judgment—in a domain that should have remained virgin. ... You fool,

don't laugh. Virgin, that is sterile. But you wanted a pillar, a shaft, a phallus present—an upright bulk. Well, it's here. You saddled me with that hunk of congested meat, that milksop with wrestler's arms. He may look like a strongman at a fair, but you don't realize how fragile he is. You stupidly forced him on me because you felt yourself ageing. (1966: 53)

The imagery situates Arthur within the sexual economies of the play. Her use of the word "phallus" calls attention to the symbolic value of the physical anatomy within the social order. In *Gender Trouble*, Butler offers analysis of the Lacanian term "phallus." She explains:

Women are said to "be" the Phallus in the sense that they maintain the power to reflect or represent the "reality" of the self-grounding postures of the masculine subject, a power which, if withdrawn, would break up the foundational illusions of the masculine subject position. In order to "be" the Phallus, the reflector and guarantor of an apparent masculine subject position, women must become, must "be" (in the senses of "posture as if they were") precisely what men are not and, in their very lack, establish the essential function of men. Hence, "being" the Phallus is always a "being for" a masculine subject who seeks to reconfirm and augment his identity through the recognition of the "being for." (1990: 61)

Butler elucidates how the function of the phallus maps onto both Irma's and Arthur's roles. While Irma's position is to facilitate the reflection, Arthur serves other's illusions until he finds himself having more utility as a corpse than an actor. At the end of the scene, a bullet punctures the Grand Balcony and lodges in Arthur's head.

Arthur's death shifts the relationship between the world internal to and external from the Grand Balcony. While the brothel serves as a space to curate, imagine, and retreat from the material demands of the revolt happening in the city, the stakes of that distance intensify when the antagonistic and permanent violence enters the space. Scenes 6 and 7 of the play bring members of the revolt in contact with the figures in the brothel. The scenes establish the specificity of both worlds and their mutual entanglement. The discussion of a coup d'état in Scene 6, which would include the death of the Queen and the Chief of Police and overtaking the Grand Balcony, produces a break from the all-encompassing world of the brothel. While the gunfire that interrupts the first five scenes of the play, and ultimately kills Arthur, calls attention to the danger that surrounds the Grand Balcony, Scene 6 gives voice to the rebels. In the scene a prostitute who has quit the brothel, Chantal, discusses the progress of the revolt with Roger, a revolutionary.

Although the revolutionaries are interested in reordering society, they understand that material change relies on the trafficking of ideas. Chantal must be transformed from a former prostitute into an idol, an image worth fighting for. Roger explains,

> A hundred women. A thousand and maybe more. So she's no longer a woman. The creature they make of her out of rage and despair has her price. In order to fight against an image Chantal has frozen into an image. The fight is no longer taking place in reality, but in the lists. Field azure. It's the combat of allegories. None of us know any longer why we revolted. So she was bound to come round to that. (1966: 57)

Although under a different context, the trafficking in women remains fundamental to the sexual economy in the city and related to the history of gendered hierarchies. This history emerges in the medieval period's expression of church doctrine that excludes women from full participation in leadership roles, through the Renaissance's presentation of women on stage that can only be played by young men, to the Enlightenment's period's understanding of the relationship between the mind and body and the characterization of women being more highly embodied. Finally in the modern period, women emerge as objects of domination in Genet's play. The shift from prostitute to idol exists along a spectrum of women's embodiment that perpetuates her function as a being for others. Her transformation from individual to symbol, "a creature they make of rage and repair" demonstrates how materialization occurs through psychic structures.

The revolutionaries are able to kill the queen and seemingly topple society; the Envoy reaches the Grand Balcony to report before Chantal and the other revolutionaries arrive. The Envoy reports that the Queen and other governmental officials have met their death and in so doing remarks on the pleasure still available within the brothel. Irma corrects, however, that the presence of Arthur's corpse disrupts the function of the house of illusions. She says, "It's make-believe that these gentleman want. The Minister desired a fake corpse. But this one is real. Look at it: it's truer than life. His entire being is speeding towards immobility" (1966: 61). The material intrudes upon the function of the fantasy and calls attention to the primary desire to transcend death and the pull of the mortal body. To live as an idol provides an ability to outlive the body and its mortal cling. The performance also demonstrates how the symbolic enables the incorporation of experience that unfolds in the Grand Balcony and helps the participants to process the destruction that occurs throughout the city. The introduction of a corpse nevertheless undercuts the primary function of the Grand Balcony as a location to escape death and its distribution through the quotidian unfolding of life.

Facing the peril of a new social order, the residents of the Grand Balcony do what they do best—they produce an illusion that will forestall material demise. In response to the revolutionaries overthrowing the government, the characters stage a reappearance of the Bishop, the General, and the Judge, the Hero, and the Queen. While the revolutionaries have worked to create a new source of ideological desire in Chantal, the known roles are too powerful. Given the option for a Queen, even if it is not "the" Queen, the citizens opt to maintain the social order. The ability of the characters to step into the governance roles so easily demonstrates the malleability and rigidity of the role. On the one hand, it seems, with some training, anyone can play the role of Queen or Bishop but, they must appear in ways that are familiar and consistent with the previous holder of the role. Therefore, physical appearance or the form of presentation matters more than the content. Similarly, once Chantal, the seeming new idol, appears on the Balcony, she suffers the fate of an uncertified substitute. In the scene, "Chantal appears, The Queen bows to her. A shot. Chantal falls. The General and the Queen carry her away dead" (1966: 70).

The return to order includes a deeper investment in the illusions at the heart of the brothel. The final scene of the play features the characters preparing for their reign with a photo shoot. The Chief of Police remarks, "After all, I want to carry on the fight by boldness of ideas as well. It was this: I've been advised to appear in the form of a gigantic phallus, a prick of great stature ... " (1966: 78). The distinction between representational and embodied experience will come to full force when Roger appears as the Chief of Police. Realizing that he has been unable to dismantle the brothel he reasons, "If the brothel exists and if I've a right to go there, then I've a right to lead the character I've chosen to the very limit of his destiny ... no, of mine ... of merging his destiny with mine ..." (1966: 93). Carmen tries to usher Roger out the establishment but he *takes out a knife and, with his back to the audience, makes the gesture of castrating himself"* (1966: 93). His blood spills everywhere, but his act does not have the desired effect. The role of the Chief of Police remains intact, calling attention to the limits of substitution, the psychic process of replacement of one object, idea, or role with another one. Substitution could be a failed act like a slip of the tongue or a deliberate displacement motivated by attachments or refusal that results in this case in the injury of the person but not of the role.

As in the religious rituals of penance, the act may function to recall a previous sacrifice but it will always fall short of the original act. Just as the substitute cannot exceed the original act of sacrifice, the Chief of Police cannot intervene in the dynamic set forth through the act of sacrifice. Roger does, however, prompt the Chief of Police to consider how he will immortalize himself. Instead of continuing to enshrine his power through ruling, he decides to encase himself in the brothel for 2,000 years to prevent an additional test of his staying power. The brothel itself remains even as all of the characters are ushered out and the audience members are asked to leave the theater. Irma comforts, "You must now go home, where everything—you can be quite sure—will be falser than here," calling attention to the ways that all appearance occurs through structured looking (1966: 96). At the same time, her comment calls attention to how the dynamics of the mirror stage exceed the house of mirrors that serves as the setting of the play. The alienation at the heart of the desire that turns to profit in the Grand Balcony also contributes to the sexual economies that govern the body in day-to-day life as well. As the third case study will clarify, however, the sexual economies are also driven by intersecting histories of race that challenge the singularity of gender and primacy of masculinity in psychoanalytic formulations.

Case Study 2: *Angels in America*

The Balcony presents ineffectual political performance. While the characters may suffer and die, their physical pain and decay have no permanent impact on the ideologies that structure their world. The setting of the brothel emphasizes the extraction of physical labor without the transformation of individuals. The play suggests that change may only occur at the individual level. Even the death of another person has limited effect on the ideology that shapes the society. Tony Kushner's *Angels in America: A Gay Fantasia on National Themes* offers a different perspective on human agency, coming after the revolutionary change of the Civil Rights movement,

Black independence, third-wave feminism, and gay and lesbian activism. The play, set in New York City in the 1980s, takes place during the height of the AIDS epidemic in the United States. In 1981, clusters of AIDS cases began to emerge among gay men in Los Angeles, New York City, and San Francisco. The disease caused widespread panic because experts did not know how it spread but they knew that, at the time, it was lethal. It also quickly became associated with populations that had historically suffered discrimination and neglect. In 1982, the Center for Disease Control (CDC) identified risk groups as the "4 Hs": hemophiliacs, heroin uses, homosexuals, and Haitians. The CDC included Haitians in the grouping because some of the first cases detected in the United States were among Haitian immigrants. While, as we now know, no ethnic group has a higher risk for the disease, the categorization produced terror and discrimination.

The stigma already attached to gay and Haitian people as well as drug users slowed responses to the disease. And while, as Sarah Schulman writes in *The Gentrification of the Mind*, our twenty-first-century perspective may wrongly remember the AIDS epidemic as something Americans collectively responded to and remedied, the truth is that activists had to demand the right to medical care and the epidemic continues today. After listening to a story on National Public Radio in the early 2000s that sought to offer a history of AIDS epidemic, Schulman reflected:

> This is the first time I've heard AIDS being historicized, and there is something clean-cut about this telling, something wrong. Something... gentrified.
>
> "At first America had trouble with people with AIDS," the announcer says in that falsely conversational tone, intended to be reassuring about apocalyptic things. "But then, they came around."
>
> I almost crashed the car.
>
> *Oh no,* I think. *Now this.* Now after all this death and all this pain and all this unbearable truth about persecution,

suffering, and the indifference of the protected, *Now,* they're going to pretend that *naturally, normally* things just *happened* to get better.

That's the way we nice Americans naturally are. We *come around* when it's the right thing to do. We're so nice. Everything just happens the way it should.

This? I realize the way one realizes that the oncoming train is unavoidable and I'm stuck on the track. *This is going to be the official history of AIDS?* (2012: 2–3)

Kushner's *Angels in America* sought to document this history and must be remembered as a controversial play due to its subject matter and its intervention in the official history of the disease and in American theater. The play made visible lives that were considered negligible (see Román 1998: 204–5). *Angels in America* not only presents individuals with the power to change their contexts, it also depicts individuals wrestling with death.

The play presents the ultimate form of physical and psychic negation, death, as negotiable. Weaving together the stories of individuals from different political, religious, racial, economic, and cultural backgrounds, the two-part play presents how the disease acts as a great equalizer. The play uses dreamscapes, hallucinations, and interactions between the living and the dead to draw together characters that otherwise would not connect. Through constant attention to the impending shadow of death and the way the disease disrupts the lives of all the characters, the central figure, Prior Walter must learn how to reconfigure his community in order to support his desire to live as his body withers away. The physical decline of the central character occurs within a play that requires extraordinary stamina of the audience and actors. The running time of *Angles in America* (Parts 1 and 2) spans seven hours and thirty minutes to eight hours, making the plays a whole-day affair. In this case study, I consider how the play engages with Foucault's theories of power and his understanding of the individual's relationship to institutions. Ultimately through the presentation of the diseased body, the play calls attention to the body as a structure as a permeable and historically specific as any institution.

Post-Structuralism and *Angels in America*, Part I: *Millennium Approaches*: Discipling Unwieldy Bodies

Angels in America begins with a funeral so as to introduce the fragility of life, the belief systems that govern life, and the contexts, rituals, and communities that reinforce those systems. In the opening scene of the play, there is a funeral for the grandmother of one of the central characters, Louis. Serving as a doubled site of mourning, the funeral depicts Louis grappling with the loss of his grandmother and learning that his lover Prior is HIV-positive, a diagnosis that in 1985 (the time setting for the first part of the play) carried a likely death sentence. Confronted with his own mortality, Louis searches for answers from Rabbi Isidor Chemelwitz presiding over his grandmother's funeral. Seeking forgiveness for "the crimes" he "may commit," Louis inquires, "what does the Holy Writ say about someone who abandons someone he loves at a time of great need?" The Rabbi, bemused, responds: "Why would a person do such a thing?" Louis explains, "Because he has to. Maybe because this person's sense of the world, that is will change for the better with struggle ... maybe that person can't, um, incorporate sickness into his sense of how things are supposed to go. Maybe vomit ... and sores and disease ... really frighten him, maybe ... he isn't so good with death" (1992: 25). The play engages with theories of post-structuralism by demonstrating how disease rearranges and exposes power relationships. While as Foucault writes, the disciplined body conceals the operation of power, the body suffering with disease becomes unwieldy and more difficult to control.

Instead of attempting to reshape the body, a strategy that Prior deploys later in the play, Louis attempts to create a barrier between himself and sickness. Louis's question, solely based on self-preservation (which, as the play unfolds, proves to be his most distinctive attribute), also brings striking attention to the deterioration and decay that accompanies growing older in general and that finds acceleration through disease. Similar to the titular character in *Everybody* who realizes, as death draws nigh, that the body will ultimately betray you, Louis must contend with the quick and visible impacts of death and disease in the dark purple Kaposi Sarcoma (KS) lesions on Prior's skin. Just as the lesions sprout onto the skin, *Angels in America* suggests that attempts at implementing artificial borders will not protect the characters from death and disease.

The play draws attention to how HIV and AIDS disrupt plans, political agendas, life expectancy, history, and family. The diseased body interrupts the ordered world of the thinking subject governed by laws and provides space for the human body to speak back to the orders that attempt to contain it. Rabbi Chemelwitz tires quickly of Louis's inquiry reminding him, "Catholics believe in forgiveness. Jews in Guilt" (1992: 25). The comparison foregrounds Louis's general investment in order, rules, the law, creating the context for progress or at least how things "are supposed to go." While a character in the play affirms, "Even hallucinations have laws," this disease rearranges governing agreements among partners about care and community (1992: 102). Through its engagement with HIV and AIDS, *Angels in America* illustrates how the disease fractured relationships and pathologized gay identity.

The structure of the play, shifting quickly from one scene to the next with characters from one community overlapping with those from another, facilitates the challenge *Angels in America* makes to traditional ideas of family and community formation. Addressing a disease primarily associated with the gay community, the play intertwines lives of gay and bisexual men and other community members in an elaborate web that demonstrates the lengths not only Louis but many will go to sustain their version of life and family. After the eulogy for Louis's grandmother, the play quickly shifts to a conversation between two attorneys: the McCarthyist lawyer Roy Cohn and closeted homosexual Mormon and Republican law clerk Joe Pitt. The historical figure Roy Marcus Cohn served as Senator Joseph McCarthy's lawyer during hearings in 1954 that investigated suspected communists. In the play, Roy and Joe are both men that sleep with men. The scene introduces their shared but vastly different expressions of conservatism, which drives the repression of bodily desires. Roy for political reasons and Joe for religious ones seek to discipline their bodies, or at least the perceptions of their sexual activities, to align with their belief systems. The play then jets to a conversation between Joe's wife Harper and a hallucinatory figment of her imagination, Mr. Lies. Harper suffers from a pill addiction that makes her prone to hallucination. The juxtaposition of scenes highlights how the medical industry institutionalizes bodies and governs action from the HIV patient to the addict. The anxiety over the unruly body in the age of HIV spreads throughout the cast, calling attention to the tenuous hold of the normative disciplined body. How does the play position the spectator's body in asking him or her to sit for an exorbitant period of time? How does the spectator relate to the nonnormative bodies that people the world of the play?

Similar to the shadow relationships between the enslaved and the white people that produce mixed race children as depicted in *The Octoroon*, many of the characters in *Angels in America* (Part 1) have connections that they are unwilling to fully acknowledge. The play reveals these connections through juxtaposition, overlapping, and the mixing together of scenes. Fully embracing theatricality, Scene 7 features Prior "at a fantastic makeup table, having a dream, applying the face." Although Prior has done some of his better work applying his makeup, he confesses, "I look like a corpse. A corpsette. Oh my queen; you know you've hit rock-bottom when even drag is a drag" (1992: 31). Harper interrupts the dream and the gender-bending performance to figure out how Prior has entered her hallucination. His presence and presentation disrupt because, according to Harper, "Imagination can't create anything new, can it? It only recycles bits and pieces from the world and reassembles them into visions" (1992: 32). Before the two delve more deeply into how their meeting across hallucinatory dreamscape rearranges the laws of knowledge production, they recognize that this space also offers heightened insight. Harper knows that Prior is "really sick" and Prior reveals, "Your husband's a homo" (1992: 33). The two, of course, must amass more evidence before they believe what has been revealed, not because they lack sufficient grounds to support the claims but because the revelation does not fit into their understanding of how the world should work. The body, in pain or pleasure, puts pressure on the desired order, rearranging longing and calling forth new social organizations. The structure of the play—first in juxtaposing groupings and, ultimately, by having them bleed into one another—facilitates the rearrangement of the sociality at the heart of the play. Instead of conceding to the purported stability and impermeability of social structures (familial, medical, legal), the characters learn how they participate in shaping them.

Since this volume has focused on how belief systems, religious or philosophical, shape the body and its appearance on stage, the family serves a primary function in its presentation. Certainly the age of empire laid the groundwork for the centrality of the family, instantiating social orders of race and gender that reappear through familial transfer, but the full blooming of that system emerged in the aftermath of trans-Atlantic slavery, the destruction of the twentieth century's two world wars, and on the heels of postcolonial movements. Each historical juncture marked a turning point for the appearance of the body within new geopolitical orders. The opening of *Angels in America* refers to the Holocaust in the Rabbi's description of Louis's grandmother:

> She was ... (he touches the coffin) ... not a person but a whole kind of person, the ones who crossed the ocean, who brought with us to America the villages of Russia and Lithuania—and how we struggled, and how we fought,

for the family, for the Jewish home, so that you would not grow up *here*, in this strange place, in the melting pot where nothing melted. Descendants of this immigrant woman, you do not grow up in America, you and your children and their children with the goyische names. You do not live in America. No such place exists. Your clay is the clay of some Litvak shtetl, your air the air of the steppes—because she carried the old world on her back across the ocean, in a boat, and she put it down on Grand Concourse Avenue, or in Flatbush, and she worked that earth into your bones, and you pass it to your children, this ancient, ancient culture and home. (1992: 10)

The Rabbi describes the process of immigration and Jewish immigrants' inability to assimilate into America, "the melting pot where nothing melted." Through the process, he details how exiles sought to secure the family. He suggests that the movement of people from villages in Russia and Lithuania changed the idea of America and transformed the streets of Brooklyn and the bodies of their occupants to sites of transition, places of passage. From one generation to the next, the old world passes into the culture and home. In *Black Movements*, I distinguish between inheritance as a practice that lays claims to the subject and affiliation, which the subject actively creates. It is through the logic of inheritance that family shapes the body, but *Angels in America*, like many late-twentieth century plays, disrupts the idea of inevitably passing down, leaving room for new generations to engage with and disrupt embodied inheritances (2017: 14).

Epistemologies of the Body: In Relationship to but Not Dependent on the Past

In the play, Prior's disease—"the disruption" of the functioning of his body—gives him access to other ways of knowing, other structures that enable him to connect with people across time and space. In *The Cultural Politics of Emotions*, Sara Ahmed argues that "emotions are intentional in the sense that they are 'about' something: they involve a direction or orientation towards an object .... The 'aboutness' of emotions means they involve a stance on the world, or a way of apprehending the world. ... Emotions are both about objects, which they hence shape, and are also shaped by contact with objects" (2014: 7). Building on Ahmed's analysis, as I explain elsewhere, "emotions circulate through and awaken shared feelings in subjects and objects, thus changing distinct individuals into collectives" (2016: 338). While Kushner's play focuses on how the medical industry structures the experience of bodies, it also calls attention to how the body accesses different forms of knowledge, different epistemologies—ways of knowing—when placed on the outskirts of these institutions.

Through the remnants of a nightmare, on the cusp between wake and sleep, Prior comes face to face with prior Priors. In the scene "a man dressed in the clothing of a 13th-century British squire" appears on Prior's bedside table (1992: 85). The man introduces himself as an ancestor Prior Walter V, who is accompanied by a Prior Walter from the seventeenth century. Together, the historical Priors come to prepare the way for the contemporary Prior to assume his role as a Prophet, with the ability to not only engage with the past but also to make claims on the future. In the play, the ancestors come to guide the main character along his path, but he has another plan in mind, one which disrupts the social script of family as a legacy routinely marked by naming practices. In response to thirteenth-century Prior's assertion that he is alone, Prior corrects, "I'm gay" (1992: 86), changing not only his familial position but the idea of family and inheritance more generally. While the main character's ancestor assumes collectivity depends on a biological connection, Prior offers a different understanding of family. The reorganization makes visible the ways genetic similarities have been used (as we saw in *The Octoroon*) to structure kinship. While Prior's haunting serves to call attention to how the past makes claims on the present, the return of the dead in *Angels in America* also has a reconciliatory function that differs from the ones celebrated in the Christian pageants of medieval drama. Instead of the dead person returning to atone for the mishaps of the wanton body, here the dead return to settle with the living.

In a different context, Roy faces a figure from his past, but one he knows very well. On his deathbed, he comes face to face with Ethel Rosenberg, a communist that Roy helped to convict of spying during the Cold War. Ethel and her husband Julius were sentenced to death and executed in 1953. The demise of the physical body, whether through disease or state disciplinary structures, does not determine the theatrical life of these characters. Adding another layer of understanding to the capaciousness of life and death as concepts, and echoing the Police Chief in *The Balcony,* Ethel and Roy discuss his impending physical death from AIDS after Ethel indicates that the ambulance operator has placed her on hold:

Ethel Rosenberg   They said a minute.

Roy   I have all the time in the world.

Ethel Rosenberg   You're immortal.

Roy   I'm immortal. Ethel. (*He forces himself to stand*)
I have *forced* my way into history. I ain't never gonna die.

Ethel Rosenberg (*A little laugh, then*)   History is about to crack wide open. Millennium approaches. (1992: 112)

Roy's claim on history depends on the political power that he has amassed. Ethel's response portends new understandings of history and its impact on the present that will provide new ways of apprehending the experience of events and bodies in relationship to but not dependent on the past.

While ghosts have appeared in Western drama from *Hamlet* to the present, the idea that power, through institutions, shapes the body as the vessel of life emerged most forcefully in post-structuralism and particularly the writing of Foucault. Rather than understanding certain privileged bodies, those of saints on kings, having the ability to transcend death, Foucault argues that individuals began to understand that their place in history depended on reconfiguring power structures and their place within them. No simple task. An early exchange between Roy and his doctor reveals that Roy understands his ability to defy the discriminatory logics of heterosexism as a function of his proximity to power, specifically his friendship with the First Lady of the United States. Kushner suggests via Roy that one does not simply decide to shift his or her social position; it requires buying into and participating in the logics of exceptionalism that a gifted and particularly industrious individual may defy the social norms and ascend in terms of class and status. When Roy says, "I have *forced* my way into history. I ain't never gonna die," he calls attention to the structures that would otherwise have limited his access if not for his political machinations. Unfortunately for Roy, the structures, in this case history, that produce his singularity also facilitate his disposability. Ethel's return suggests that the historical order has been disrupted and just as disease prematurely claimed the lives of many people during the AIDS epidemic, the experience of the disease, as Prior's response to his ancestor suggests, made different ways of life possible and in so doing reshaped history or, in the words of Ethel, cracked it wide open. The historical shift accompanies a change to physical reality marked by the reappearance of the dead, the reanimation of bodies and the return of the repressed violence that Roy enacted in order to gain political power. Roy's "way into history" depended on domination of people, gay and communist, that he must ultimately reckon with in his final hours.

Roy may have been able to force his way into history, but he cannot determine how he will be remembered. In many ways, Roy's notion of historical immortality corresponds to the idea of America as an egalitarian country that would not adhere to the social hierarchies of the old European countries. American's investment in imperialism would more closely align it to its European counterparts, even though the national rhetoric of equality and the Declaration of Independence that "all men are created equal, that they are endowed by their Creator with certain unalienable Rights, that among these are Life, Liberty and the pursuit of Happiness" seem to support the independence movements of the postcolonial period in African, the Caribbean, and Latin America. This duality plays out in Louis's one-sided assertion that "in a country where no indigenous spirits exist—only the Indians, I mean Native American spirits and we killed them off so now, there are no gods here, no ghosts and spirits in America, there are no angels in America, no spiritual past, no racial past, there's only the political, and the decoys and the ploys to maneuver around the inescapable battle of politics" (1992: 92). The inability to see America as both an empire and a rhetorical bastion of independence puts pressure on how the body and body-politic appears. The play depicts a much more complicated web of power that enables Roy to hide that he is a conservative that spews homophobic rhetoric, sleeps with men, has contracted HIV, and at the same time that he cannot escape the devastating role he played in facilitating "the Red Scare."

To prepare for the relationships that will form in Part 2 of the play, Part 1 depicts a split scene that features Louis and Prior and Harper and Joe. In the overlapping scene both Louis and Harper discuss leaving. This scene recalls the previous one in which Prior enters Harper's delusion. This intrusion enables greater clarity about their social positions: Prior must face the gravity of his disease and Harper must confront her husband's sexuality. Both moments of revelation occur in a trance-like state. Through the interactions across scenes, the characters enter into new couplings that help advance the play and call attention to how family and history will change as millennium approaches. The discussions of leaving offer insight to the audience of the characters' misperceptions rather than greater clarity to the characters themselves. The conversations between Louis and Prior and Harper and Joe focus on how deception has undermined the relationships. Returning to the theme of appearance versus materiality, Harper and Prior challenge the idea that Joe and Louis can love as they live lives filled with lies. By the end of the scene both Louis and Harper vanish: Louis simply leaves and Harper departs with her drug-induced guide, Mr. Lies. Their departures make more permeable the distinction between the real and supernatural. Instead of staging the transcendence, and therefore superiority, of the spiritual, the play depicts the physical body's ability to move between planes. The movement calls attention to how perception shapes and materializes the body. Calling into question our presumptions about the material facts of the body, the movement highlights the body's malleability and permeability. Instead of suggesting as *The Balcony* does, that individuals overestimate the capacity for physical transformation, *Angels in America* depicts characters underestimating these abilities. The play puts pressure on understandings of the body as a decaying shell if the body, unlike in *Everybody*, remains after death. The individual's ability to retain the body, even after its demise, foregrounds the power of the individual will.

Angels in America, Part II: *Perestroika*

The mixing of worlds that portends a new order of things in *Angels in America*, Part 1, takes on greater magnitude in Part 2 with not only the intrusion of individuals from the past and present into the characters' lives, but also shifts in the environments that the characters inhabit. How does history and the environment set the stage for understanding the body as fixed? What happens to the body when we set history and the environment in motion? The second part of the play opens "In the Hall of Deputies, The Kremlin. January 1986" with an elderly Bolshevik asking what governmental structure will succeed the Soviet Union (1993: 13). He questions how the former Soviet Union will survive in the new social order: "(A little pause, then with sudden, violent passion:) And Theory? How are we to proceed without *Theory*? What system of Thought have these Reformers to present to this mad swirling planetary disorganization" (1993: 13–14). His statement situates political theory on a continuum with religious belief systems that have long organized cultures and shaped people. Different schools of thought contribute to an ecosystem that attempts to fix the body in place rather than understand it as constituted through ideas. The Elderly Bolshevik offers a metaphor that highlights how theory produces material realities, shaping the lives and experiences of people. He says, "If the snake sheds his skin before a new skin is ready, naked he will be in the world, prey to the forces of chaos. Without his skin he will be dismantled, lose coherence and die. Have you, my little serpents, a new skin?" (1993: 14). Theory here serves as cover, an external wall that protects or leaves individuals vulnerable. While different systems are possible, the fable suggests a structure must be in place or chaos will ensue. The chaos emerges, however, out of an antagonistic relationship between the snake and the world. The snake's new skin not "being ready" poses a problem because it leaves the animal vulnerable. But the fable does not allow for the possibility of that vulnerability resulting in a dismantling that is also a putting back together. The possibility for subsequent rearrangement of understandings of the human body as not necessarily reproductive but interwoven in history and community motivates Prior's quest. The second part of the play calls attention to historical narrative as a permeable structure that, following Foucault, has a history that facilitates power relationships.

The scene then shifts dramatically to reveal that we are in Prior's bedroom where an Angel hovers over his bed and invites him to begin his work as a Prophet. The movement from the Kremlin to Prior's bedroom not only transforms his intimate space but brings the state order into the bedroom demonstrating how sexual politics inform state policies. The play also bridges the gap between the political battles in the mid-twentieth century over communism and in response to the burgeoning gay rights movement. An outgrowth of the Cold War and the intermingling of the "Red Scare" with the "Lavender" one, Prior must now chart the way forward and figure out how to produce a new skin—a barrier with connective tissue that brings order to the entire physical and political body.

In a scene seemingly worlds away and yet still in the New York City setting of the play, Harper imagines that she has transported to Antarctica with Mr. Lies, a travel agent that comes to her aid with escape plans also facilitated by her drug use. Dealing with a very familiar war between body and mind, Harper contemplates how her heart has broken and yet she still lives. She also wonders how she can long for Joe even after he has betrayed her. The paradox of intellectual and emotional desires begins to come into greater focus when she realizes that the contradictions of her heart match the ones of her physical space. Although she thinks she is in Antarctica where she is freezing cold, she opens the scene holding a pine tree and then realizes there are no trees in Antarctica. By the time she recalls retrieving the tree from the Brooklyn Botanical Garden, the police have come to arrest her. Although Harper does not want to accept her reality, there are laws that constrain it. She cannot love her illusion of Joe just as she cannot transform Brooklyn into Antarctica. The way forward requires theory that is responsive to material realities of the past and present but that also understands theory's ability to transform reality.

The delicate interplay between calling forth new understandings of the body and cultivating delusions emerges through the distinction between characters such as the Angel that appear and intrude on Prior and those that central characters summon like Mr. Lies. Mr. Lies presents an attempt to escape the material realities of Harper's relationship with Joe while the Angel represents a call to transform the social order, to produce a new skin, the first an act of deception, and the other an act of invention. In *Angeles in America*, unlike *The Balcony*, retreating to a world of lies marks false hope rather than ingenuity. The way forward in Kushner's play requires contending with and shaping the impact of the past in order to create space for unruly bodies that speak back to the disciplinary regimes that repress nonnormative relationships.

The blending of earthly and supernatural realities allows for the aligning of mythic force with phallic imagery. When the Angel returns in Part 2 to set Prior on his mission, he has a physical response. The Angel instructs Prior to locate spectacles and a book buried in his apartment. After some convincing, he does so and then asks, "Wait. Wait. (*He takes off the glasses*) How come ... How come I have this ... um, erection? It's very hard to concentrate." The Angel responds, "The stiffening of your penis is of no consequence" (1993: 39). She continues to explain that "The Body is the Garden of the Soul" (1993: 40). Prior and the hermaphrodite Angel have sex to produce an "Angelic orgasm" that "makes protomatter, which fuels the Engine of Creation" (1993: 41). In this revision of Biblical myths, the body becomes the source of renewal rather than sin. In addition, creation does not rely on heteronormative coupling.

Repurposing the body and pleasure offers a new entry point to the relationship between physical and intellectual acts. The Angel explains, "In Creating You, Our Father-Lover unleashed Sleeping Creation's Potential for Change. In YOU the Virus of TIME began!" (1993: 42). Rather than locating salvation through penance and external redemption, the Angel explains that God created man with the potential to change and therefore to redeem himself. The implication of choosing Prior and locating that change through sex has as much to do with the reclamation of the diseased body through pleasure as his sexuality. Nevertheless, the play attempts to disrupt heterosexism by making the Angel's sex nonbinary. The shift in guiding myths from religious to secular takes on full force through the characterization of Prior and the depiction of him as a Prophet. The play ties his vision to his physical decay and through his proximity to death, he is able to perceive more clearly. Reversing the relationship of the body to the mind through his experiences of suffering, Prior gains a deeper understanding of history and the potential for life rather than the mitigation of the physical. His body serves as the landscape for his revelation.

Psychoanalysis and the Abject Body

Prior's condition offers him a new level of insight and the unlikely couplings in the play enable him to make sense of his new visions. How does the familial rearrangement in the play challenge traditional notions of family? How do they challenge what Sigmund Freud saw as primary psychic attachments (that is, between parent and child) and allow for alternative forms of desire to enliven the characters? After Louis leaves Prior, Louis begins a relationship with Joe who has abandoned Harper. Joe's mother, Hannah, comes to New York to try to support Harper and understand her son's choices. Along the way, she meets Prior and they form a friendship. Although Prior recovers from the sickness that invades his body and threatens his life in Part 1, he does not maintain his treatment and his condition worsens again to the point of hospitalization. Hannah accompanies a crestfallen Prior to the hospital. She instructs, "Just lie still. You'll be all right" (1993: 103). He responds: "No. I won't be. My lungs are getting tighter. The fever mounts and you get delirious. And then days of delirium and awful pain and drugs; you start slipping and then. I really ... fucked up. I'm scared. I can't do it again" (1993: 103). Eschewing his panic, she concludes, "You shouldn't talk that way. You ought to make a better show of yourself" (1993: 103). Uncomforted, Prior laments, "Look at this horror. (*He lifts his shirt; his torso is spotted with three or four lesions*) See? That's not human. That's why I run. Wouldn't you? Wouldn't anybody?" (1993: 103). The familiar physical manifestation of HIV—KS lesions—functions like a scarlet letter, or, following the writing of psychoanalytic critic Julia Kristeva, a sign of the abject.

In *Powers of Horror: An Essay on Abjection*, Kristeva explains abjection as the casting-off of objects that threaten the subject in order to distinguish between life and death. She states, "The corpse, seen without God and outside of science, is the utmost of abjection" (1982: 4) and also writes,

A wound with blood and pus, or the sickly, acrid smell of sweat, of decay, does not signify death ... No, as in true theater, without makeup or masks, refuse and corpses *show me* what I permanently thrust aside in order to live. These body fluids, this defilement, this shit are what life withstands, hardly and with difficulty, on the part of death. There, I am at the border of my condition as a living being. (1982: 3)

While Prior interprets the presence of the lesions as a sign of his abjection, Hannah offers a different account. She counters, "It's a cancer. Nothing more. Nothing more human than that" (1993: 103). The association of KS lesions with HIV as an apocalyptic judgment of the gay community provides one explanation for the disease, a historical narrative that positions the LGBTQ community as deviant. Prior's rendering reflects the plague-like effect of the disease in the late twentieth century; although, with adequate health care, individuals can now live with HIV, in the 1980s it often promised a death sentence. Because the disease affected populations considered disposable, research into treatments and cures were slow to emerge. Prior only recovers from his first hospitalization because a friend, a nurse, steals medicine from Roy who has been able to secure the then experimental antiviral medication azidothymidine (AZT) due to his governmental contacts. Resources and access, as in most cases, determine what bodies will live and which will die. But in the play access becomes complicated and permeable due to the unlikely couplings like the friendships between Prior and Hannah, which offers Prior a different understanding of how historical narrative shapes the body.

The play animates the circulation of power through relationships that develop across communities and shows how power shapes the relationships. Prior, an HIV-positive man, meets Hannah, a devout Mormon, and she becomes part of the family that he chooses. Although she believes in biblical teachings in response to Prior's trepidation that the Angel will revisit him, she reminds Prior, "An angel is just a belief, with wings and arms that can carry you. It's naught to be afraid of. If it lets you down, reject it. Seek for something new" (1993: 103). On the interpersonal level, many of the main characters in the play suffer through betrayal by the people on whom they most depend. The social structures that secure individuals have frayed. At one point Prior quips to Hannah, "I wish you would be more true to your demographic profile. Life is confusing enough" (1993: 102). His expectations must shift to enable the support that he needs, which includes letting go of those that have let him down and investing in new relationship that can support him. The metaphysical imagery of the play points to a shift in thinking from the mind and spirit having dominion over the body, and shifts further when Hannah suggests that the body's manifestation inform how we understand the spiritual realm. *Angels in America* offers the possibility for revolutionary change, knowing people's lives depend on it. The play offers an ideological response to the medical apparatus of who lives and who dies by rethinking familial attachments.

In *Angels in America*, Prior's rejection of physical deterioration's correlation with diminished life expectancy coincides with his challenge to "the word" having dominion over life. In the final exchange between Prior and the Angel in Heaven, the Council Room of the Continental Principalities, Prior tells the Angel and the Principalities that he does not want the Book found in his apartment floor. Instead, he wants his blessing. He says, "Even sick. I want to be alive" (1993: 131). The Angel consoles, "You only think you do. Life is a habit with you. You have not *seen* what is to come: We *have*: What will the grim Unfolding of these Latter Days bring? That you or any Being should wish to endure them?" (1993: 131). The Angel's warning does not deter Prior or convince him of redemption in foregoing bodily suffering. Prior understands the physical desire drives the compulsion of life that challenges the Angel's argument. He requests:

Bless me anyway. I want more life. I can't help myself. I do. I've lived through such terrible times, and there are people who live through much much worse, but ... You see them living anyway. When they've more spirit than body, more sores than skin, when they're burned and in agony, when flies lay eggs in the corners of the eyes of their children, they live. Death usually has to *take* life away. I don't know if that's just the animal. I don't know if it's not braver to die. But I recognize the habit ... Bless me anyway. I want more life. (1993: 133)

Prior's statement puts pressure on the primacy of "the word" in Biblical teaching. He foregrounds how the body poses a challenge to the intellect and the will, even as the body's appearance, "more sores than skin," calls forth rhetorical histories and medical diagnoses. Prior's prophecy culminates with the reclamation of the body and its thirst for liveness. While *The Balcony* located that liveness primarily in the world of illusions, Prior finds it in laying claim to the diffuse power structures that depend on habitual action for their support. The illusion is that individuals do not have a choice. While the circumstances of decision-making may be so dire that the choice amounts to a nondecision, the act of asserting oneself still functions to disrupt the invisible circulation of power and reclaim bodily desires.

Case Study 3: *Fathers Come Home from the Wars,* Parts 1, 2, and 3

Just as *Angels in America* troubles what encompasses the "real" world, Suzan-Lori Parks's *Father Comes Home from the Wars*, Parts 1, 2, and 3, questions the totality of another major social system—slavery. First performed at the Public Theatre in New York in 2014, the main character's journey draws from the Odyssey. The play, set in the midst of a war, features characters named Homer, Penny, and Ulysses. In this play, the war is the American Civil War, and most of the parts of the play take place on a plantation in West Texas. Hero must decide in the play whether he should stay at home or fight for the Confederate slave holding states in the war. In Parks's play, similar to Kushner's play, challenging prevailing beliefs does not signal delusion; it offers reprieve from oppression. Post-structuralist thought enables conceptions of working outside the frame of seemingly totalizing systems such as slavery. The seemingly straightforward choice—stay or go—masks a much more complicated set of choices that specify life as human property. Ultimately, Hero's choice, which really amounts to a non-choice because either way his labor will be in the service of the institution of slavery, calls attention to how Black people's agency, familial relationships, and bodily control only occur in spaces that are outside of regulated society—underground, off the map, or outside of time.

As detailed in the Introduction, "performance" accounts for the repetition embedded in action and the power such repetition wields, the accumulation of action over time produces the impression of permanence rather than choice. Some actions become so familiar that they contribute to identity categories such as male or female, what scholars call "performatives." Blackness, and racial identity more broadly, requires a rethinking of theories that use repetition and its accumulative time to establish identity (see Colbert, Jones, and Vogel 2020). As suggested by the analysis of *Angels in America*, Part 2, historical narratives may be contested and engaged. As a result, understandings of identity do not only emerge through repetition but also through contestation, revision, and disruption. *Father Comes Home from the Wars* invites an understanding of the Black body engaging in the performance of fugitives, runaways, figures on the run from the law, and fugitive performance—twice-behaved behavior that locates Blackness outside normative ideas of gender, race, and sexuality.

As Hortense Spillers argues in "Mama's Baby, Papa's Maybe: An American Grammar Book," the trans-Atlantic slave trade marked Black people's exclusion from the symbolic order of Western culture (Spillers 1987). Because Black people existed as both humans and commodities, transferability, or what Saidiya Hartman and C. Riley Snorton call fungibility, was ascribed to the enslaved's existence. As I state in the introduction, fungibility may be defined as the status of the Black body resulting from white people's ability to categorize the bodies of the enslaved by projecting meaning, value, thoughts, and desires onto them even in precise opposition to Black peoples' lived reality. Snorton explains, "Fungibility became a critical practice-cum-performance for Blacks in the antebellum period. To suppose that one can identify fugitive moments in the hollow of fungibility's embrace is to focus on modes of escape, of wander, of flight that exist within violent conditions of exchange" (2017: 57). The enslaved not only contended with the constant proposition of being sold or having their labor sold but also the possibility of "stealing" themselves by running away or participating in practices that did not increase their use value, such as reading, having sex for pleasure, or participating in art practices. When thinking of embodied actions, twice behaved behaviors, as the production of the self, one must recalibrate to account for a system that renders self-possession theft. In this context, any performance becomes fugitive, because it places the enslaved in violation of the laws that relegate Black people to property. *Father Comes Home from the Wars* depicts enslaved people in pursuit of self-possession and freedom.

Fugitive Performativity

In order to draw forth the fugitivity that will become Hero's third option (to stay, to go, or to run away) the play first establishes the prevailing order. The first line reads, "How much time we got?" (2015: 5) and introduces a set of comments throughout Part 1 that mark time. When day breaks at the close of Part 1, the cyclical nature of time emerges as a point of tension with the linear dynamic of past, present, and future. Instead of going somewhere, the enslaved characters seem caught in a vicious loop that situates any choices that they make in service of their domination because "time is still owned by the Boss-Master" (2015: 12). The play evidences this dynamic by revealing that Hero contemplates fighting for the Confederacy because if he goes to war his master has promised to free him. Old Man, one of Hero's advisors, a father-like figure, pinpoints the emptiness of the promise: "The great Boss-Master-Boss give you your freedom of choice. Like he figures his freedom of choice is gonna somehow Take the place of the Rightful Freedom that he's been denying you" (2015: 19). Old Man calls attention to the distinction between making a choice and acting as a free subject that determines the parameters of decision-making. If Blackness may only operate within a closed loop of domination, then its ability to function as a performative challenges normative values. The bodily will, the idea of individual agency, that functions as the promise of performance meets its limit point in Blackness.

The play, however, suggests another option. As the characters continue to discuss what Hero should do, his friend, Homer disabuses them of their notion of choice. He clarifies:

> ... you shouldn't be doing neither.
> Cause you should'd stoop—
> To do neither
> Cause both choices, Hero,
> To stay here and work the field
> To go there and fight in the field
> Both choices are
> Nothing more than the same coin
> Flipped over and over
> Two sides of the same coin
> And the coin ain't even in your pocket. (2015: 42)

The flipping of a coin, which implies a fair chance, actually amounts to a rigged system. Since Hero has no bodily autonomy, he has no choice. He may only access choice as a fugitive or a runaway. In the passage, Parks returns to the metaphor of gaming that she explores in her earlier play *Topdog/Underdog* (2001) to challenge understandings of individual's relationships to structures that offer the possibility of change. The only way for Hero to access choice is through the destruction of slavery as a system not by making a decision within that system.

As I describe in the Introduction, Butler, following Foucault, explains that individuals have limited ability to transform the discursive structures that regulate their identity through repeated behaviors that become concretized over time. Anticipation, repetition over time, and duration produce the effect that is gender. Altering such an effect would require a concerted effort enacted collectively across time and circulated through a different set of desires. In Parks's play, Blackness short-circuits the relationship between behavior and discursive structures because Black people do not have the power to name themselves free subjects under the law. Therefore, even if Hero decides to fight for the Confederacy, the choice amounts to an affirmation of the given legal and national systems and not a revision to them. The efficaciousness of Black-embodied action requires reframing the contexts of its expression. Or, as Moten explains, "Racism is neither being, nor anonymity, nor universality ... it is rather, the power that responds ... to ... these fugitivities, these flights" (2018: 24). Moten situates "fugitivities" or what I call fugitive performance as actions that call attention to the fissures in institutionalized racism, in this case the system of slavery. Slavery as a system retains its power by convincing Hero and other enslaved that there is no alternative system. Fugitive performance—running away, passing, and stealing—demonstrates the possibility of another structure based in Black people's self-possession.

Homer proposes instead of making a choice to stay or to go that Hero work outside the system. He clarifies,

> That man will never free you. Ever. You're waiting for him to give you Freedom When you should take it ... Mark it, now's the time. Start running and you'll be free so quick

The War will still be raging and Master will be promising
Freedom to the next fool Fool enough to believe it. And
you, You'll have your Freedom already. Taken. Taken for
yourself It'll be completely yours. (2015: 43–4)

Homer offers an option that will take Hero off the grid and
into a different temporal configuration because it will be
governed by his affirmative position, a position he cannot
occupy within slavery. Homer's suggestion would redefine
Hero from enslaved to fugitive—the escaped slave, the outlaw,
the subject of police violence and brutality (see Best and
Hartman 2005). It would also require, as Snorton suggests in
the introduction of this section, that Hero take on a posture
of flight. His life would require a perpetual state of covert
movements that would shield his body from being detected
by slave catchers. In so doing, it would render him invisible
within the institution of slavery and no longer subject to
its definitions. Fugitivity offers an alternative trajectory
for defining Blackness in terms of performance because it
disrupts the power dynamic between the performer, history,
and interpreter. Instead of the performer acting in relationship
to a history consolidated as a performative, a recognizable
category affirmed through repeated action, the performer
explodes the former category and situates himself within a
new one. In so doing, Blackness becomes disentangled from
only being understood through the logics of slavery and
therefore property relationships.

The rearrangement enables the visibility of alternative
familial structures and responds to past injuries. In the play,
Old Man refers to himself as Hero's "fake-father" because
they are not biologically related. Within the logics of slavery
as depicted in *The Octoroon*, however, biological ties do
not necessarily determine family when they cut across racial
lines. *Father Comes Home from the Wars*, Part 1, complicates
these social laws further by advancing a notion of family
that one chooses. These connections are visible outside of the
institution of slavery and offer an insight into what fugitivity

enables in terms of self-definition. Before Homer weighs in on Hero's choice, we learn that the second time Master offered Hero his freedom was in exchange for punishing Homer for running away. Hero punishes Homer by cutting off his foot. Anticipating that there will be a physical price to pay for not going to war, Hero asks Old Man and his lover, Penny, to cut off his foot. Neither can bring themselves to do so and the exchange draws attention to the mutability of the Black body under slavery. The level of injury possible belies any idea of choice. To understand the time of fugitive movements that shape Blackness outside of the white gaze, one must begin with a rupture that may result in death but that also is necessary for freedom.

Father Comes Home from the Wars, Part 2, depicts Hero supervising a Union solider that the Colonel captured. Its plot turns when Hero realizes that the Union Solider, Smith, is not a white officer; he is a Black Private. Similar to the conversation that animates Part 1, Smith and Hero discuss freedom as a choice informed by visibility and recognizability, particularly the physical markings of Blackness. In Part 1, Hero struggled with the idea that his freedom could function independently of his Master's sanction. In Part 2, Hero confronts the same paradox of freedom as only available in fugitivity, as a criminal within a legal system that defines person as property. The Colonel confirms this perspective, quoting Hero: "'Master,' he said, 'running off, well, that would be the same as stealing', he said" (2015: 67). In the context of slavery, that theft would be of labor and property. As *The Octoroon* clarifies in the auction scene, the enslaved and their labor belong to the estate. *Father Comes Home from the Wars*, Part 2, intensifies the implications of the laboring body in service of a system that denies any hope of freedom by transferring labor from the plantation to the Civil War battlefield.

Part 2 also returns to the question of truth claims at the heart of Part 1. The Colonel promises "Freedom for [Hero's] Service, isn't that right?" (2015: 82). Hero concurs, "You gave your Word on it," even though all of his labor already belongs to the Colonel (2015: 82). How can Hero barter or strike a deal with the Colonel for something, his labor, that he does not own? Hero's ability to make good on the promise would require that he resituate himself as a subject, but, as Saidiya Hartman's *Scenes of Subjection* elucidates, fugitivity is the only subject position available for the enslaved. She explains, "Criminality is the only form of slave agency recognized by the law. Thus the fashioning of the subject must necessarily take place in violation of the law, and consequently, will, criminality, and punishment are inextricably linked" (2015: 41). She clarifies that when an enslaved person commits a crime, for example, she becomes a subject within the law but only in that case. Otherwise, she has no rights that the law will uphold. Therefore, as Parks's play makes clear, the autonomy that emerges by way of Enlightenment thinking does not translate to the enslaved.

Part 2 explores this paradox as it pertains to market value and draws attention to how capitalism interferes with the Enlightenment humanism that remains the basis for US democracy. Capitalism's interference with egalitarian notions of democratic choice continues to inform how the Black body circulates on and offstage even into the twenty-first century. After Hero deduces that Smith is passing for a white officer (recall passing at the heart of *Plessy v Ferguson*), he questions: "How much you think we're gonna be worth when Freedom comes? What kind of price we gonna fetch then?" (2015: 95). Failing to anticipate the afterlife of slavery and how it will continue to produce race as a hierarchy, Smith responds, "We won't have a price. Just like they don't. That'll be the beauty of it" (2015: 95). Smith and Hero talk across one another. Hero asks Smith about worth, about their value within capitalism and Smith comments on appearance: "We won't have a price" (2015: 95). Not having a price does not translate to not having a relative value. The question of value relates to ideas about ownership assumed by Enlightenment definitions of subjectivity. In the context of the enslaved, the only way to animate these dynamics is to steal oneself. Hero attempts to help Smith understand, saying "Where's the beauty in not being worth nothing?" (2015: 95). Of course, Hero is only willing to determine freedom as a gift the master bestows which then positions him to continue to determine value. The institution of theater perpetuates and draws attention to the dynamic of autonomy as a gift, something that is given rather than something that you take, that limits Black people's ability to appear. The history of slavery short-circuits the accumulative principle because it produces a racialized distinction between human beings and subjects. The idea that meaning accrues through white subjects repeated performances over time renders the white and Black body in service, at least partially, to white viewers' whims and will.

Smith underscores the persistence of race as a determining factor for freedom when he factors in capitalism. He muses,

> Maybe even with Freedom, that mark, huh, that mark of the marketplace, it will always be on us. And so maybe we will always be twisting and turning ourselves into something that is going to bring the best price. That's the way we were born into this, so is it always gonna be like that for us, slavery or not? Freedom or not? Are we ever going to get us a better place in the marketplace? (2015: 98)

The staging of Blackness holds a unique conceptual space in racial histories because it epitomizes how visibility enabled Black people to be both valueless and exceptionally valuable, all within the logics of the marketplace. In the context of the laboring Black performing body, the spectrum of representation from the auction block to the virtuoso performer (think Michael Jackson or Beyoncé) demonstrates how Black people have been able to get a place in the marketplace while remaining within a system of nonvalue. The only way forward that Smith can deduce is "a place besides just the auction block. And maybe that starts by stealing yourself. Steeling yourself, making yourself like metal on the inside. Maybe it'll get better from there. But, I don't know" (2015: 99). The place requires a different mode of self-fashioning that does not depend on the logics of the marketplace and the value that attends via accumulative logics of appearance.

Parks's play returns to slavery to reroute understandings of Blackness in and as performance. The play hints at these dynamics by making the passing character one of the more radical figures rather than a tragic one. In Part 3 of *Father Comes Home from the Wars*, characters again consider staying or leaving, but it focuses on two of the central characters that Hero leaves behind when he goes to war, Penny and Homer. With the encouragement of three runaways, Homer tries to convince Penny to leave with him. Since Hero's departure, Homer and Penny have consummated a relationship that has resulted in her pregnancy. Nevertheless, Penny feels tied to Hero and does not want to leave knowing he may return. Although all evidence suggests that Hero prioritizes himself above all other relationships and that Penny loves Homer, she remains attached to the idea of Hero.

Each part of the play considers how embracing fugitivity, the body as the stolen property of the enslaved rather than a commodity of exchange for the master, requires letting go of an idea or ideal that seems to have as much force as physical restraints. Part 3 attempts to disrupt these investments with the return of Hero's dog Odyssey. Upon his return, the enslaved try to determine if Hero has died on the battlefield. Understanding that whatever response he offers will cause dissatisfaction, Odyssey offers tangential commentary on the idea of a "Master":

When I say my Master of course I'm speaking of Hero. Him and you all have a Master, but his and you all's Master is not my Master. Although you could say that, because the Boss-Master owns Hero who in turn owns me, you could figure that the Boss-Master is in fact my Master. But he is not. Although, the Great Master, the one who sits in the sky, you know, the Great Master is Boss-Master's Master and Old-Hero's Master and my Master too, but that Colonel-

Boss-Master is not my Master. When the Colonel called me, I would never ever come. (2015: 130)

Odyssey's comments depict how an animal, in the eyes of twenty-first-century law a piece of property, may refuse a human and respond to another human that also circulates as property. Not only does Odyssey clarify that he does not answer to the Colonel, he also challenges the implicit hierarchy produced through property relations. Odyssey suggests that the individual must yield in order for authority to function. The power of refusal animates the possibility of recalibrating these positions and gives them their force. It also calls attention to how human and nonhuman bodies assert themselves in systems of domination. Although, as we will learn by the end of Part 3, Hero, who returns from war as Ulysses, has taken a wife and does not care for Penny, she will not refuse him until he denies her first.

The social hold of position coincides with a historical one that the play emphasizes. As in Part 1, time of day is a recurring theme in Part 3. When asked if they will leave, characters respond: "Not dark enough. / Not dark enough. / Not dark enough to jet / Not yet" (2015: 136). The characters know that the dark of night will ease running away. They do not know, however, that Abraham Lincoln has issued the Emancipation Proclamation and that the Colonel is dead. As a result, they do not need to depend on the passing of day into night to offer cover for escape, the historical tide has turned. But the play asks, what difference does historical change make if those impacted by the shift do not know or believe it? Within the time span of Part 3, the enslaved characters transform to free subjects, but does that change their appearance in the play, for the audience? At the same time, Hero returns with a new name and uniform but his old selfish ways. How does his renaming change how he appears? In the final part of the play, Penny and Homer run off with the runaways, which triggers a shift. They leave not knowing about the Emancipation Proclamation and, therefore, they take their freedom, choosing to live off the grid and underground rather than within a system that does not recognize them. Suspending the logics of slavery, the final act of defiance redefines the characters. Through their actions they reshape the appearance of their bodies but in so doing also obscure them. The coupling of affirmative action and masking distinguishes and triangulates Black performance. The play draws on racialized histories depicted in *The Octoroon* and *An Octoroon* to suggest that Black performance gains some of its force from inscrutability. Rather than primarily shifting understandings of power dynamics, a technique at the heart of post-structuralism, Black performance must, in part, short-circuit the system to reposition the actors.

Section 2 has explored how theories of the body shift following the Second World War to account for changes in how we understand human agency. Section 2 considered how the key historical periods of the Civil War, the Second World War, and the AIDS epidemic enable understanding the materialization of the body through acts of human agency. Finally, Section 2 revisited a central question of the volume: how does one distinguish between the real and the fake, by complicating the distinction between the material reality of the body and the discursive regimes and histories that shape it? Whether human or nonhuman, the philosophical developments of the late-twentieth and early-twenty-first centuries open the door for theater theories of the body in environmental, transgender, and disability studies.

SECTION THREE

Porous Bodies: New Interpretations

Introduction

The focus on nonnormative identities (i.e., gay, Black, sick, woman) in the late twentieth century destabilized the uniformity of the disciplined body. By focusing on nonnormative individuals, theorists and playwrights began to understand the body as porous and unruly rather than fixed and self-contained. Building on the work of Black studies, feminist, and queer theories of the body, scholars in environmental studies, transgender studies, and disability studies developed theories of the body as a part of an ecology rather than a singular closed-off entity. This section considers how humans become intertwined with other organisms and systems to produce a linked fate. How do normative histories of gender create binaries and what are other ways of understanding gender at the intersection of race and sex? How do normative bodies prescribe understandings of embodiment through physical presentation, movement, and interaction? In burgeoning theater theories of the body, the interconnected nature of human life is emphasized whether with other humans, different species or the planet we share. Coming to terms with how the human body functions as a porous organism animates many new theoretical conversations in the field.

Environmental Studies and the Body

William E. Connolly argues in *Climate Machines: Fascist Drives and Truth* (2019) that the earth has been understood either as the docile recipient of human action or in a reciprocal relationship with human actors. The comparison assumes either a vertical relationship that represents human domination of other life forms, a top-down hierarchal system, or a horizontal relationship predicated on exchange. A vertical arrangement draws from structuralist philosophies or as existentialist philosopher Albert Camus writes in *The Rebel* (originally published 1956), "For the Christian, as for the Marxist, nature must be subdued" (1984: 222). Connolly says a horizontal

> image of species evolution encourages less hubristic practices of science than those advanced today by proponents of climate geoengineering, cloning, nuclear physics, behavioral social science, neo-Darwinism, and—most generically—the pursuit of human mastery over a docile earth. It rather encourages scientists to watch and study life forms to gauge the multiple strivings, resonances, horizontal intersections, and bifurcation points through which evolution proceeds. A bifurcation point issues at least one if and one course actually taken. Sophocles would call it a crossroad. (2019: 31)

The idea of life forms having reciprocal impact takes up great urgency in the midst of the world's climate crisis and the global pandemic produced by the Covid-19 virus.

Environmental studies questions the relationship between humans and ecologies. Pushing the theoretical question to the extreme and following the work of Jane Bennett in *Vibrant Matter: A Political Ecology of Things* to distinguish between human beings and other forms of matter. She explains:

> This habit of parsing the world into dull matter (it, things) and vibrant life (us, beings) is a "partition of the sensible," to use Jacques Rancière's phrase. The quarantines of matter and life encourage us to ignore the vitality of matter and the lively powers of material formations, such as the way omega-3 fatty acids can alter human moods or the way our trash is not "away" in landfills but generating lively streams of chemicals and volatile winds of methane as we speak. (2009: loc 48)

Bennett's language may recall Fred Moten's distinction between commodities and commodities who speak, drawing attention to a period in Western history in which Black people were not accorded the distinction of "vibrant life." Bennett's description also evokes pre-enlightenment theories of the body as matter in service to or needing the discipline of the mind. Attending to the vitality of matter creates a spectrum for better understanding the body. Bennett concurs, "The philosophical project of naming where subjectivity begins and ends is too often bound up with fantasies of a human uniqueness in the eyes of God, of escape from materiality, or of mastery of nature; and even where it is not, it remains an aporetic or quixotic endeavor" (2009: loc 76). Environmental studies situates the human body as a part of an exchange with other matter rather than in a transcendent position to matter.

At the same time, human beings dominate other nonhuman animals based on their ability to reason and produce culture. The consumption of animals marks human's willingness to dominate other species. Bennett asks, "What difference would it make to public health if eating was understood as an encounter between various and variegated bodies, some of them mine, most of them not, and none of which always gets the upper hand?" (2009: loc 61). Yoking the human to an antagonistic dualist relationship with either other animals or the earth prevents understanding the human as a historical category associated with the privileged position of European, able-bodied, men. Connolly says a horizontal understanding premised on human interconnectedness would also consider "how life could have emerged from nonlife" (2019: 32). This is the question at the heart of fugitive studies as referenced in Section 2 (see Spillers 1987; Moten 2003; Snorton 2017; Best and Hartman 2005) and one that animates Nick Dear's adaptation of Mary Shelley's nineteenth-century novel, *Frankenstein*. In 2011 London's National Theatre produced Dear's adaptation, which emphasizes the entanglement of human beings with other species through the interchange between Victor Frankenstein and the Creature he cobbles together. The intimacy of the human body with the world it has wrought comes to the fore in the production through the interchangeability between man and man-made figure. Given Frankenstein's creation, where does the human end and the cyborg or non-human animal begin? How does the human body appear differently when fantasies of a human uniqueness are abandoned?

Case Study 1: Nick Dear's *Frankenstein*

The opening scene of Dear's *Frankenstein* calls attention to the Creature's construction and interconnectedness between his human creator and the physical remains used to create him. The stage directions indicate:

> Light: the Creature has got down from the frame. He squats on the floor. He seems confused. He has no speech and his movements are erratic. Spurts of blood come from the sutures in his skin. It goes dark again. Now we realise what's happening: it gets light when he opens his eyes. The Creature seems to realise this too. He puts a hand clumsily

to his eye. He holds it open. It stays light. He lets his hand
fall and his eye closes again. It gets dark. With both hands
he forces his eyes open and holds them open. (2011: 3)

Although the Creature does not retain control of his
environment throughout the play, his ability to manipulate
lightness and darkness establishes a world of entanglement.
Still unhealed from the operation that forms him—a suturing
together of human waste scavenged from cadavers—his
stitches leak as the Creature comes to realize that he is in
control of the theatrical space. The movements of the actor
determine the lighting for the audience, shifting from a
spectacle brightened by the stage lights or enshrined in
darkness. The shift—from darkness to light and back again—
calls attention to bodies in space and how the environment
responds to the movements of the central character. This
entanglement, which Connolly also locates in Shelley's novel,
reframes the notion of human agency and asks audiences
to consider not only our impact on the environment but its
impact on us. Connolly contends, "Entangled humanities
extend the reach of care without contending that the species
life of human beings—in its vast variety of circumstances—
is unimportant" (2019: 41). Focusing on entanglement
extends care because the emphasis shifts from the individual
to the relationship. One must understand the ripple of the
Creature's impact. This is a radically different understanding
of the world than that presented in Genet's *The Balcony*.
Like much mid-twentieth-century drama *The Balcony*
contemplated individuals' limited control and impact. In
Dear's *Frankenstein*, Victor makes the Creature from the
leftover parts of other dead human beings. He builds a new
species out of remains, one that he ultimately cannot control.
Whereas in *The Balcony*, humans only had control over their
life and death, in the world of *Frankenstein* a nonhuman
animal has the ability to disrupt the status quo, reordering
his own life and the humans that he engages.

The National Theatre production emphasizes not only
mutuality but also interchangeability with the casting decision

to have Benedict Cumberbatch and Jonny Lee Miller alternate the roles of Victor Frankenstein and the Creature through the production's run. Both casting and plot emphasize the interdependence of the two figures but one would have to see multiple performances to fully realize the impact of casting on how the play conceptualizes the relationship between, and not the singularity of, the human and the creature. The National Theatre's digital collection (hosted by Drama Online) does provide the opportunity to experience performances of both actors in both roles. The play chronicles the creature's development from a nonverbal experiment into a sentient speaking figure with a startling, and, based on the reaction of other characters, grotesque, physical appearance. Throughout the play, the people who interact with the Creature have violent responses to him based on his physical appearance. It is not until he meets a blind man, DeLacey, that he finds any empathy. The blind man cares for the unnamed protagonist and teaches him to read. DeLacey bonds with the Creature because he shares with him a nonnormative body. Being differently abled, DeLacey does not immediately react to the Creature's physical differences.

The National Theatre production depicts cultural development at odds with nature, foreclosing the environment as a source of wonder. In the play, DeLacey's son and daughter-in-law strive to become farmers but find the soil rocky and unyielding. Because of his compassion, the creature secretly clears the field so the couple can plant crops. In another scene as DeLacey begins to teach the creature to read using John Milton's *Paradise Lost*, the pupil becomes raptured by falling snow and spellbound by the moon. The choice of Paradise Lost, an epic poem that recalls the Biblical story of the fall of man, the temptation of Adam and Eve in the Garden of Eden, and the story of Satan, a fallen angel, calls attention to the hubris of man and supernatural being alike. It also foregrounds the idea of human physical desire, eating from the tree of knowledge, as the species' fundamental flaw. The play challenges the antagonism between the mind and body by disrupting the singularity of the human as a thinking thing.

The Creature's penchant to feel connected to the environment and to relate to nonhuman matter sets up an understanding of matter more generally, including the human body, as interdependent with its surroundings rather than subject to them. DeLacey encourages the Creature to disregard the snow and asks why he finds the moon so mystifying. The Creature explains that he and the moon share a similar solitary existence, a shared experience of isolation. The shift in perspective reflects an understanding of mutuality key to environmental studies of climate crisis (2019: Connolly, *Climate Machines* and *Cultivation and Catastrophe*). Considering the source text for the play, Connolly asserts, "Sublime and volatile forces inform the world of *Frankenstein* because Mary Shelley was alert—like Sophocles before her—to how multiple nonhuman forces and agencies can infuse, disrupt, inspire, and pummel human life" (2019: 36). This understanding of shared fate also informs many feminist and ethnic studies projects (*This Bridge Called My Back, After the Party, The Black Shoals,* and *Black and Blur*). Tiffany Lethabo King's *The Black Shoals* uses the metaphor of the shoal—a submerged ridge, bank, or bar, to describe interconnected systems of knowledge production in Black studies. She explains:

> The shoal, like Black thought, is a place where momentum and velocity as normal vectors are impeded. It is the place where an adjustment needs to be made. As an in-between, ecotonal, unexpected, and shifting space, the shoal requires new footing, different chords of embodied rhythms, and new conceptual tools to navigate its terrain. The shoal enables this book to shift its conceptual lens to a liminal space between the sea and the land. (2019: 4)

The ecological metaphor serves as a fertile example of how knowledge emerges in a relationship between two distinct bodies, in this case the land sentiment and the ocean. In the play, the Creature's unwillingness to create a hierarchy between nature and culture enables his ability to appreciate his position in the world.

Following the Creature's lament about his isolation, the National Theatre production stages a dance sequence to express the Creature's dream of finding a mate that will understand his unique circumstances. Throughout the play, the Creature's appearance and physical presentation distinguish him from humans. At the beginning of a performance with Cumberbatch cast as the Creature, he jerks about, bending his body to emphasize that he has just gained facility in movement, even though he is the size of an adult. The imagined dance scene similarly depicts the woman making frantic movements, but her physical expression is more targeted and sequenced. At the end of their choreographed duet, they embrace and when the woman wraps her arms around the Creature it overwhelms him. The dance sequence emphasizes how physical presentation, in terms of the characteristics of the body and comportment, informs one's appearance as human. Touch produces a physical connection that calls attention to the body as a source of information and a site of isolation. Being together becomes materialized through the choreography of the dreamscape.

Although Butler's work focuses on how individual action contributes to how we understand gender and the body, her argument focuses on the pull of history and desire rather than interactions between individuals. The emphasis in Butler's *Bodies That Matter* and *Gender Trouble* is on how embodied action informs perceptions of the body and gender as historical ideas. In her analysis the pull of history not only advances normative desire but also the power dynamics that adhere therein. Carrie Noland offers analysis to account for the body in motion, arguing in *Agency and Embodiment*, "kinesthetic experience, produced by acts of embodied gesturing, place pressure on the conditioning a body receives, encouraging variations in performance that account for larger innovations in cultural practice that cannot otherwise be explained" (2009: 2–3). Connolly's work and Dear's play invite us to consider how actions, particularly interactions, shape the body and call attention to other networks beside historical ones that call the body forth. These may include racial, cultural, geographical, and biological (in the organic sense or as relating to organisms) networks that do not necessarily follow an accumulative model of formation.

Although DeLacey helps the Creature to understand his dream and learn about good and evil, he cannot do the same for his children. Once the blind man's children find their father's guest, they attack him. With a newly formed understanding of human relationships the Creature retaliates. As he says, "What do they do when they feel like this? Heroes, Romans—what do they do? I know. They plot. They revenge. I sweep to my revenge!" (2011: 29). The Creature burns the blind man's house to the ground and all three inhabitants with it. In the staging of this scene, the antagonism that forms in the moment of self-realization animates the creature's relationship to Frankenstein and how they interact upon his return to his birthplace. The critical turning point depicts how the idea of the human in Western thought as emblematized by *Paradise Lost* requires an enmity.

The play depicts the creature returning to Geneva with a demand that Frankenstein respond to the isolation the doctor produced by creating him as the only one of his species. The Creature commands Victor to make him a mate. The antagonism that develops between Victor and the Creature may seem to resemble Hegel's master/slave dialectic, which serves, according to Alice Rayner as a "model of otherness within the same, taken from [Hegel's] famous image of the relation between mere consciousness (associated with the body) and self-consciousness as a master/slave dialectic" (2002: 549). In Hegel's rendering, two independent self-consciousnesses encounter one another and engage in a life-and-death struggle for recognition. The struggle persists because in domination the master cannot receive the recognition he seeks from the slave. At the same time, the master must dominate the slave to maintain their relationship.

Conversely, the struggles between Victor and the Creature reflect a horizontal relationship of bacteria feeding on an enabling body because the two exist in an antagonistic reciprocal relationship. Frankenstein and his creation have a series of confrontations that stage their mutual need and interdependence; even though they are at odds, they require each other. Although rooted in antagonism, need also draws them together. Therefore, complete domination would not benefit either party. In their first confrontation, Victor does approach the Creature as someone or something to conquer. The Creature charges, "Why did you abandon me?" (2011: 38). And the doctor responds, "I was terrified—what had I done" (2011: 38). The Creature questions if transforming waste into life, however grotesque, gave the doctor pause. Victor affirms and counters, "Well, now I have come to take it away" (2011: 38). Victor attacks the Creature but he is no match for his creation. He has lost control. His inability to dominate the creature shifts their dynamic and sets in motion a series of confrontations that solidifies their bond but also serves to theorize the underlying necessity of entanglement, drawing attention to the dependency of bodies on nonhuman animals and matter.

Once Victor realizes that he cannot dominate his creation, more Satan than Adam as the creator describes, the fallen angel of his creation narrative, he makes a deal with the Creature that has the potential to proliferate the humanlike bodies. Their argument details the shift from the language of a master-slave antagonism to an understanding of their mutual imbrication. Notably, this understanding coincides with a recourse to reason as the distinguishing characteristic and, therefore, foundation of human dominance:

Creature   You alone have the power to—

Victor   Create another brute—another monster?
No, I will not, I—

Creature   It is my right!

Victor   You have no rights. You are a slave. You want me to make you a female, so the pair of you can be wicked together? No, I will not. Torture me as much as you like, I'll never consent! (2011: 41)

Calling forth the distinction between human and enslaved depicted in *Father Comes Home from the Wars*, *Frankenstein* establishes that subjectivity translates to being subject under the law, but in the world of the play the Creature has the ability to challenge the regulations. Linking subjectivity to human consent, *Frankenstein* also suggests who qualifies as human under that same law. Even though Victor attempts to foreclose the rights of the Creature, the Creature has the ability to cause Victor physical pain. Similar to how power structures animate the interaction in *The Balcony*, even characters that do not have access to structural protection may exercise their will. In this case, however, the character takes a nonhuman form.

The Creature, having already demonstrated that he can withstand Victor turning physical force against him, now establishes what he has learned from the people that have taught him, like Caliban, how to curse:

Creature   I will not torture you. I will reason with you. Isn't that what we do? Have a dialogue?

Victor   There is no dialogue with killers!

Creature   Yet you'd kill me if you could! Why, you have just tried! So why is your killing justified, and mine is not?

Victor   I won't argue with you! My God, I'm halfway up a mountain, debating with a—a—

Creature   A living creature! (2011: 41)

Although Victor understands that he has produced this dynamic, he did not anticipate that his creation would turn against him. The position of the Creature also mimics interdependence in nature that produces an organism, once safe, that mutates into something dangerous. The play, however, allows the Creature to make a moral distinction, questioning humans having the singular capacity to live. Although humans do not have the unique capacity, calling attention to that misunderstanding shifts the philosophical stakes from a focus on human agency at the center of existentialist concerns and mid-century Western theater and the dynamic between the two characters, which reflects an understanding of the human as part of an ecosystem.

Stating the political claims of her project to explore the assertive force of matter, Bennett explains:

> Why advocate the vitality of matter? Because my hunch is that the image of dead or thoroughly instrumentalized matter feeds human hubris and our earth-destroying fantasies of conquest and consumption. It does so by preventing us from detecting (seeing, hearing, smelling, tasting, feeling) a fuller range of the nonhuman powers circulating around and within human bodies. These material powers, which can aid or destroy, enrich or disable, ennoble or degrade us, in any case call for our attentiveness, or even "respect" (provided that the term be stretched beyond its Kantian sense). The figure of an intrinsically inanimate matter may be one of the impediments to the emergence of more ecological and more materially sustainable modes of production and consumption. (2009: loc 90)

The intractable battle emerges out of Victor and the Creature's pursuit of domination. When Victor refuses to acknowledge the Creature with mutual respect because of his physical differences, he places them in a death battle that will result in mutual destruction.

Victor, being challenged at every turn, takes recourse to what he knows, but the Creature has been taught well and knows how to counter:

> **Victor**   A nothing, a filthy mass of nothing! I am your master, and you should show respect—
>
> **Creature**   A master has duties—you left me to die! I am not a slave. I am free. If you deny my request I will make you my enemy, I will work at your destruction, I will dedicate myself, I won't rest until I desolate your heart! (*Pause.*) I apologise. I did intend to reason. (2011: 43)

In the staging of the scene, the Creature physically attacks Victor. Showing the how physical actions secure relationships, the Creature's expression of force functions as a counter to Victor's propensity to act as a master. The scene ends with a handshake to seal the deal, a conventional gesture of physical proximity. In *Homo Necans: The Anthropology of Ancient Greek Sacrificial Ritual and Myth*, Walter Burkert explains this gesture established an agreement through the choice to suppress aggression: "An agreement can be expressed quickly and clearly in words, but it is only made effective by a ritual gesture: open, weaponless hands stretched out toward one another, grasping each other in a mutual hand shake—a mutual display of aggression sealing what had previously merely been spoken" (1986: 34). The physical proximity establishes the potential for future violence without elaborating it in the moment.

Throughout the play, the characters draw attention to the antagonism that Victor's actions produce, resulting in the other character's repulsion for his creation rather than for him as the creator. This dynamic reinforces the negligibility of the body and, by association, the material world that supports human life. Like Shelley's novel, Dear's play "seems to appreciate the self-organizing capacities of nonhuman processes, as it worries immensely about wayward forces set into motion by a hubristic human creator who does not represent the multiple ways creations can morph through new experiences beyond the anticipations of the creator" (Connolly 2019: 33). In order to form the Creature's mate, Frankenstein enlists the services of gravediggers, Ewan and Rab, to find body parts for "medical research." Assuming a heteronormative dynamic even among creatures, they exhume a woman recently drowned and although Rab poses objections to the work, Ewan reminds him, "they're dead. They're not coming back" (2011: 55). This seemingly clear-cut distinction establishes a natural order that presumes human dominance and arbitration of life and death. The circulation of life and death does not, however, only pertain to when one is either in or outside of the grave. As Christina

Sharpe argues, death attaches to certain subjects because of their historical proximity to it: "In the wake, the past is not past reappears, always, to rupture the present" (2016: 9). Sharpe's description destabilizes the past. Uneven, incomplete, and parts yet undiscovered, the past emerges in relationship to the present—to the writer, reader, and artist. When the Creature happens upon the gravediggers and realizes the process of reanimation, he too finds it repulsive. He questions, "Stolen at night from wet soil? Made out of meat for the dogs? Even I can feel disgust! Will he fashion a beauty, from this filth? And will I want her, stinking of death?" (2011: 56). He suspects the smell of death will cling to his partner and, therefore, undercut his desire. The Creature sees the abject position and proximity as contrary to beauty.

The idea of fashioning a woman from remains takes on additional philosophical weight when Victor's dead brother William comes to him in a dream to ask if she will have the capacity to reproduce. Victor has already upset the social order by blurring the division between life and death. William's question prompts Victor to consider if he wants to allow other humanlike species to perpetuate outside of his control. Ultimately, Victor finds the stakes too high and decides to renege on his deal.

When the Creature realizes that Victor has resurrected a woman only to kill her out of fear that his species will grow, the Creature enacts revenge on Elizabeth, Victor's fiancée. The play suggests that the Creature rapes her and then kills her to compensate for his loss. The act of substitution continues, however, because when Victor finds the Creature with Elizabeth's corpse, instead of shooting him, he lets him escape. This kindness solidifies the relationship of host and parasite, locking the two in a continual antagonistic bond. The Creature explains, "He lives for my destruction, I live to lead him on" (2011: 78). Later in the final scene, with Victor near death, the Creature says, "Don't leave me. Don't leave me alone. You and I, we are one. (*The Creature kneels and gently cradles Victor*) While you live, I live. When you are gone, I must go too. Master, what is death? What will it feel like? Can I die?" (2011: 79) Although the Creature refers to Victor as Master, they both understand their mutuality, suggesting a shift from the Master-slave dialectic to a model of relationality that requires a different mode of recognition from the individual presumably in power, one not predicated on domination but on a shared need. The shift indicated here is from humans mastering and dominating all other species to an understanding of their linked fate with other creatures.

Given the ongoing climate crisis and the emergence of the worldwide pandemic caused by Covid-19, the ecological basis of survival has never been more apparent. At the same time, the qualities that distinguish human bodies from other matter remain in question as humans become more dependent on nonhuman forms for survival, including prosthetic devices. The interrelation of human with nonhuman matter may mark the future for the species but that future requires rethinking domination as its primary posture.

Transgender Studies and the Body

Entanglement serves as a useful frame to not only consider how different systems, including environmental, shape the body but also schools of thought. While the post-structuralist turn enabled a rethinking of identifications and identity (race, gender, and sexuality specifically as my Section 2 case studies have illustrated), Transgender Studies theorists have questioned the implications of performance theory for the trans body. In *Assuming a Body: Transgender and Rhetorics of Materiality*, Gayle Salamon takes up the relationship between the psychoanalytic theory (specifically the work of Sigmund Freud, Jacques Lacan, and Paul Schilder) and queer theory that has animated performance theories of the body. Salamon "seeks to challenge the notion that the materiality of the body is something to which we have unmediated access, something of which we can have epistemological certainty, and contend that such epistemological uncertainty can have great use, both ethically and politically, in the lives of the non-normatively gendered" (2010: 1). While Butler in *Bodies That Matter* contends that our experience of the body is mediated by a number of things including language, history, and power relationships, in trans studies the emphasis is on understanding the materiality of the body.

Salamon offers a nuanced and layered examination of how the "felt sense" of the body creates a point of theoretical intersection between different disciplinary approaches, but that "felt sense" means something slightly different in each school of thought. She writes:

> Phenomenology, psychoanalysis, and queer and transgender theory each approach the question of what it means to assume a body by asserting the primacy of a "felt sense" of the body, and the different means by which each discipline does so, when examined in conjunction, can begin to delimit the contours of this body whose felt sense is usually unquestioned. Phenomenologists understand this felt sense as proprioception, psychoanalysis thinks of it as the bodily ego, and it has sometimes emerged in transgender theory as the grounds for claims about identity and "realness." Each of these disciplines contends that this meaning, and ultimately the body itself, hinges on a felt sense. It is my contention that one can acknowledge the ways in which this felt sense is a product of, and also subject to, cultural interpretations without disavowing or dismissing the persistent importance of this sense. (2010: 2–3)

The distinction between proprioception (which draws attention to experience the bodily ego, which centers on perception) and claims for realness (which draw from conceptions of materiality) marks important differences for theories of the body. Nevertheless, *Assuming a Body* offers a way to think through these theories next to each other, ultimately to untether transgender theory from realness, or a preexisting material condition that differs from the materialization of the body, but also to consider, again, how we come to know the body. Transsubjectivity emphasizes the limits of understanding the body through its oppositional position with the mind and rather offers a theory of the body rooted in history. While Simone de Beauvoir's well-known assertion in *The Second Sex* (1949) that "One is not born, but rather becomes, a woman" is often used to understand gender formation, her observation may also apply to sex. Understanding de Beauvoir's statement in terms of sex emphasizes the interlacing of biology with history, language, and power to form the body. Consider the term "woman" applies to both gender and sex, de Beauvoir's statement calls attention to the power structures that materialize the body as much as the histories that hail gender identity.

The shift in the relationship between Frankenstein and the Creature may be understood in phenomenological terms that focus on the imbrication at the heart of the line, "he lives for my destruction. I live to lead him on." As Salamon details, "Merleau-Ponty challenges both philosophical accounts of embodiment that rely upon a dualistic conception of body and self and mind/body theorists whose conceptions of the body are predicated on starkly drawn models of inside and outside" (2010: 5). Providing an alternative understanding of relation, quoting Salamon, Merleau-Ponty "suggests that our bodies are inextricably intertwined with both ourselves and the worlds in which our bodies are situated. [Salamon] consider[s] his claim that bodies become material only through relations with others and explore[s] the consequences that this might have for theorizing transsubjectivity" (2010: 5). The context of Salamon's project, transsubjectivity, offers a helpful turning point to rethink how we come to know the body and to reconsider not only our ability to access other people's bodies but our own. *Assuming the Body* reminds us that language, history, power, and perception not only alienate us from the "real" materiality of those we encounter but of ourselves as well. Therefore, we also exist at a critical distance from what we understand our selves to be and how others see us. Moreover, the interweaving of fields of knowledge, as Salamon and Connolly suggest, allows for an understanding of how exchange factors into perceptions and experiences of the body.

Case Study 2: Branden Jacob-Jenkins's *Everybody* Revisited

As I detail in Section 1, Branden Jacob-Jenkins's *Everybody* structures exchange into the play as a means to disrupt assumptions about what roles individuals may play and how the actors bodies determine casting. In the 2019 production of the play at the Shakespeare Theatre in Washington DC, directed by Will Davis a trans man and the cast of main characters, Somebodies—Alina Collins Maldonado, Avi Roque, Kelli Simpkins, Ayana Workman, and Elan Zafir—include cis, trans, Black, brown, and white actors. Roque, a transmasculine nonbinary Latinx actor, played the role of Everybody on one of the nights that I attend the production.

As I detail in Section 1, near the end of the play the character Love has a conversation with the titular protagonist about the body. Love explains that aging often coincides with the lack of control over the body. To symbolize the lack of control, Love commands Everybody to take off all his clothes and run back in forth, mimicking an act of penance. As Ashley O'Mara notes in a review of the play, "This is supposed to be a humbling moment for Everybody. They have forgotten about Love, even though Love has been sitting in the audience the whole time. In retribution, Love literally says to Everybody: 'You could humiliate yourself a little more.' But Roque described the scene as a simultaneously 'empowering' one, and it showed. 'My body, over the span of the last two years, has gone through a lot of changes,' said Roque. 'But these are intentional decisions that I have made for myself to find more love and peace with myself'" (O'Mara 2020). As with other moments of the adaptation, the casting in the play challenges some of the essential presumptions about the body and its relationship to the human. Instead of serving as a site for discipline, Roque suggests the body as a locale of knowledge also provides the opportunity to materialize through the theatrical process. The production does not end with the reconsolidation of normative binaries but rather the openness of multiplicity signaled by the title.

Disability Studies and the Body

Disability studies in particular offers insights about the body that resonates with theories of the racialized and gendered body previously explored. Nevertheless, it is important to note that several of the plays explored in this volume feature characters that would be described as disabled or differently abled including Homer in *Father Comes Home from the Wars* (Parts 1 and 3), DeLacey in *Frankenstein*, and Prior in *Angels in America*. They all stand in distinction from what Rosemarie Garland-Thomson defines as the normate, "the figure outlined by an array of deviant others whose marked bodies shore up the norm's boundaries .... [It] is the constructed identity of those who, by way of the bodily configurations and cultural capital they assume, can step into a position of authority and wield the power it grants them" (cited in Hall 2011: loc 67). The normate has resonance with the bodily ego, but it circulates as a collective understanding rather than an individual ideal. While the ego functions in psychoanalytic terms in relationship to the individual, the normate establishes cultural and social standards and ideals. While the two inform one another, the normate renders not only Homer's body different but all fugitive bodies.

From a philosophical sense, as Kim Q. Hall argues in the introduction to her edited collection *Feminist Disability Studies*, the idea of the disabled body recalls Enlightenment debates about the relationship between the body and mind and the proper subordination of the body to the mind. Quoting feminist disability theorist Susan Wendell, Hall asserts, "The prevailing Western view ... associates normalcy with the exercise of proper discipline and control over the body. Consequently, ableism is a product of long-standing Western somatophobia" (2011: loc 97). Hall continues, "As Sandra Bartky (1990) observes in her discussion of femininity and the phenomenology of oppression, disciplined bodies are also properly gendered bodies—that is, bodies whose behaviors, features, and desires flow seamlessly from binary sex characteristics" (2011: loc 97). The regulation at the heart of categorizing bodies is in productive tension with the depiction of disabled figures in the aforementioned plays because each poses a challenge to the given order, demonstrating how theory comes to assert its force and how theater intervenes in the conversation. In the depiction of Homer as a runaway, he learns the inhumanity of slavery when his purported friend Hero cuts off his foot. DeLacey as the only figure that treats the creature as a human does so because he does not see what his children recognize as grotesque. Prior is gifted with prophesy as he begins to lose his physical sight, suggesting he has access to a future-oriented vision at the cost of his ability to see clearly in the present. The plays establish how physical difference produces social positions that offer access to different forms of knowledge. Instead of barring the characters from the world of the mind, the positioning enables them to access different ways of knowing and being that challenge the normative power associated with ableism or the bodily ideal. Disability studies, as a frame that Hall argues best offers insight in conversation with feminist studies, also finds key points of articulation with thought alongside theater studies, which has historically considered how bodily knowledge, feeling, movement, touch, produces a circuit of information with the mind (see also Kuppers 2003). The interdisciplinary approach of disability studies, modeled in Hall's book, offers a useful intervention for theories of the body, echoed and expanded upon in late twentieth- and early twenty-first-century theater.

Case Study 3: Mike Lew's *Teenage Dick*

Based on Shakespeare's *Richard III*, Mike Lew's *Teenage Dick* features Richard, a high school student with cerebral palsy. Similar to his source character, Lew's protagonist engages in a political battle for power but this one takes place in a battle for the senior class president. In the 2020 production of the play at Theater Wit in Chicago but streamed for audiences throughout the world as a result of the global pandemic, the central character used his physical specificity, the way he moved and often lost control of his body, to his advantage, eliciting sympathy and support from his teacher and classmates and, therefore, power. For example in the play Richard convinces his teacher to change the election rules so he can run for office. Similar to *Father Comes Home from the Wars* (Parts 1 and 3), DeLacey in *Frankenstein*, and Prior in *Angels in America*, *Teenage Dick* establishes how physical difference produces social positions. These positions are not preestablished but emerge in relationship to the body as an exchange between systems and the materialization of the body.

Although the nonnormative body often must contend with implicit and explicit hierarchies regarding beauty and physical appearance in theater, both *Richard III* and *Teenage Dick* show how the central figures use the presumptions about the body, those of the character's political audience, to their advantage. These sly performances recall the fugitive performances examined in Section 2, which work outside the legal and social systems that structure the materialization of the body to carve out space for cultural outcasts.

Across its three sections, *Bodies* examines the theories and practices of Western performance from the Medieval to the contemporary theater and ends with a consideration of how the strict material understanding of the body that centralizes it within the performing arts does not always fully account for the way the body operates in larger ecology with other nonanimal and nonhuman forms of matter. At the same time, the volume attends to how feminist, brown, Black, and nonnormative theater makers critique the centrality of the white normative body. As we continue to contend with environmental and epidemiological crises, the place of the human body in theory, theater, and theater theory will continue to shift and pose questions for how we map its limits. As those boundaries begin to blur, they may give way to more capacious understandings of matter as flowing between human and nonhuman bodies allowing for relationships of mutuality and care.

REFERENCES

Ahmed, Sara (2014). *The Cultural Politics of Emotion*. Edinburgh, UK: Edinburgh University Press.

Aronson-Lehavi, S. (2019). "Sexuality and Gender," in *A Cultural History of Theatre: In the Middle Ages, Volume 2*, ed. Jody Enders. London, New York: Bloomsbury Academic, 59–76.

Badham, Van (2018). "#MeToo Movement: 'Is It OK for Me to Touch You Here?': The People Making Rehearsal Rooms Safe," *Guardian*, November 13. Available online: https://www.theguardian.com/world/2018/nov/13/is-it-ok-for-me-to-touch-you-here-the-people-making-rehearsal-rooms-safe. Accessed April 22, 2021.

Bennett, Jane (2009). *Vibrant Matter*. Durham: Duke University Press, Kindle Edition.

Bernstein, Robin (2009). "Dances with Things: Material Culture and the Performance of Race," *Social Text* 27.4: 69–70.

Best, Stephen and Saidiya Hartman (2005). "Fugitive Justice," *Representations* 92.1 (Fall): 1–15.

Bevington, David (2012). "The Morality Play," in *Medieval Drama*. Chicago: University of Chicago Press, 790–5.

Boucicault, Dion (2014). *The Octoroon*. Peterborough, Ontario: Broadview Press.

Brandes, Philip (2018). "Benedict Cumberbatch and Jonny Lee Miller Take on 'Frankenstein.' But Who's the Better Monster?" *Los Angeles Times*, October 19. https://www.latimes.com/entertainment/arts/theater/la-et-cm-frankenstein-national-theatre-live-20181019-story.html Accessed January 8, 2020.

Brooks, Daphne (2006). *Bodies in Dissent: Spectacular Performances of Race and Freedom, 1850–1910*. Durham: Duke University Press.

Brooks, Helen E. M. (2019). "Sexuality and Gender: Changing Identities," in *A Cultural History of Theatre: In the Age of Enlightenment, Volume 4*, ed. Mechele Leon. London, New York: Bloomsbury Academic, 55–76.

Burkert, Walter (1986). *Homo Necans: The Anthropology of Ancient Greek Sacrificial Ritual and Myth*. Berkeley, CA: University of California Press.

Butler, Judith (1990). *Gender Trouble: Feminism and the Subversion of Identity*. New York: Routledge.

Butler, Judith (1993). *Bodies that Matter: On the Discursive Limits of Sex*. New York: Routledge.

Butler, Judith (1999). "Preface" to *Gender Trouble: Feminism and the Subversion of Identity*. New York: Routledge.

Camus, Albert (1984). *The Rebel*. New York: Vintage.

Catanese, Brandi Wilkins (2011). *The Problem of the Color[blind]: Racial Transgression and the Politics of Black Performance*. Ann Arbor: University of Michigan Press.

Césaire, Aimé (1992). *A Tempest*, trans. Richard Miller, originally published 1985. New York: Theater Communications Group.

Cheng, Anne (2013). *Second Skin Josephine Baker and the Modern Surface*. Oxford: Oxford University Press.

Colbert, Soyica Diggs (2016a). "Black Rage: On Cultivating Black National Belonging," *Theatre Survey* 57.3: 336–57.

Colbert, Soyica Diggs (2016b). "Playing the Help, Playing the Slave: Disrupting Racial Fantasies in Lynn Nottage's *By the Way, Meet Vera Stark*," *Modern Drama* 59.4: 1–23.

Colbert, Soyica Diggs (2017). *Black Movements: Performance and Cultural Politics*. New Brunswick: Rutgers University Press.

Colbert, Soyica Diggs, Douglas Jones, and Shane Vogel (2020). *Race and Performance After Repetition*. Durham: Duke University Press.

Connolly, William E. (2019). *Climate Machines: Fascist Drives and Truth*. Durham: Duke University Press.

De Beauvoir, Simone (2011). *The Second Sex*. New York: Vintage Books.

Dear, Nick (2011). *Frankenstein*. London: Faber and Faber Ltd.

Diamond, Elin (1997). *Unmaking Mimesis: Essays on Feminism and Theatre*. New York: Routlege.

Elam Jr., Harry J. (2001). "The Device of Race: An Introduction," in *African American Performance and Theater History*, ed. Harry J. Elam, Jr. and David Krasner. Oxford: Oxford University Press, 3–16.

Enders, Jody (2019). "Introduction," in *A Cultural History of Theatre: In the Middle Ages, Volume 2*, ed. Jody Enders. London, New York: Bloomsbury Academic, 1–17.

Esslin, Martin (1996). *The Theatre of the Absurd*. London: Eyre.

Eyring, Teresa (2016). "Standing Up for Playwrights and against 'Colorblind Casting'." *American Theatre*, January 7. Available online: https://www.americantheatre.org/2016/01/07/standing-up-for-playwrights-and-against-colorblind-casting/ (Accessed April 22, 2020).

Foucault, Michel (1995). *Discipline and Punish: The Birth of the Prison*. New York: Vintage.

Genet, Jean (1966). *The Balcony*, trans. Bernard Frechtman. New York: Grove Press.

Gobert, R. Darren (2013). *The Mind-Body Stage: Passion and Interaction in the Cartesian Theater*. Palo Alto, CA: Stanford University Press.

Hall, Kim Q., ed. (2011). *Feminist Disability Studies*. Bloomington: Indiana University Press.

Hegel, G. W. F. (1977). "Independence and Dependence of Self-Consciousness: Lordship and Bondage," in *Phenomenology of the Spirit*, trans. A. V. Miller. Oxford: Oxford University Press, 111–19.

Henke, Robert (2019). "Introduction: Culture, Cultural History and the Early Modern Theatre," in *A Cultural History of Theatre: In the Early Modern Age, Volume 3*, ed. Robert Henke. London, New York: Bloomsbury Academic, 1–14.

Hughes, Langston (1926). "The Negro Artist and the Racial Mountain." Available online: https://www.poetryfoundation.org/articles/69395/the-negro-artist-and-the-racial-mountain.

Jacobs-Jenkins, Branden (2015). *An Octoroon*. New York: Dramatist's Play Service.

Jacobs-Jenkins, Branden (2020). *Everybody*. New York: Theatre Communications Group.

Jameson, Frederic (1972). *The Prison-House of Language: A Critical Account of Structuralism and Russian Formalism*. Princeton, NJ: Princeton University Press.

Kristeva, Julia (1982). *Powers of Horror: An Essay on Abjection*. New York: Columbia University Press.

Kuppers, Petra (2003). *Disability and Contemporary Performance: Bodies on Edge*. Oxon: Routledge.

Kushner, Tony (1992). *Angels in America, Part One: Millennium Approaches*. New York: Theatre Communications Group.

Kushner, Tony (1993). *Angels in America, Part Two: Perestroika*. New York: Theatre Communications Group.

Lacan, Jacques (1977). "The Mirror Stage as Formative of the I Function as Revealed in Psychoanalytic Experience," in *Écrits: A Selection*, trans. Alan Sheridan. New York: W. W. Norton & Company, 75–81.

Lovell, Lucy (2018). "Blazing a Trail with the Bard: Paapa Essiedu Takes the Lead Role in a Touring Version of Shakespeare's Hamlet," *Manchester Evening News*, January 26: 5.

Marx, Karl (1990). *Capital: A Critique of Political Economy*, vol 1, trans. Ben Fowkes. New York: Penguin.

Moten, Fred (2003). *In the Break: The Aesthetics of the Black Radical Tradition*. Minneapolis: University of Minnesota Press.

Musser, Amber Jamilla (2018). *Sensual Excess: Queer Femininity and Brown Jouissance*. New York: New York University Press.

Neely, Carol Thomas (2004). *Distracted Subjects: Madness and Gender in Shakespeare and Early Modern Culture*. Ithaca: Cornell University Press.

Nicholson, Eric (2019). "Sexuality and Gender: The Early Modern Theatrical Body," in *A Cultural History of Theatre: In the Early Modern Age, Volume 3*, ed. Robert Henke. London, New York: Bloomsbury Academic, 51–70.

Noland, Carrie (2009). *Agency and Embodiment: Performing Gestures/Producing Culture*. Cambridge: Harvard University Press.

O'Mara, Ashley (2020). "Something for *Everybody*: Radical Inclusion in a Modern Adaptation," *Howlround*, February 20. Available online: https://howlround.com/something-everybody.

Parks, Suzan-Lori (2005). "An Equation for Black People on Stage" and Suzan-Lori Parks, "New Black Math," *Theatre Journal* 57.4: 576–83.

Parks, Suzan-Lori (2015). *Father Comes Home from the Wars* (Parts 1, 2, and 3). New York: Theatre Communications Group.

Purcell, Carey (2018). "Intimate Exchanges," *American Theatre*, October 23. Available online: https://www.americantheatre.org/2018/10/23/intimate-exchanges/ (Accessed April 22, 2021).

Rayner, Alice (2002). "Rude Mechanicals and the Specters of Marx," *Theatre Journal* 54.4: 535–54.

Roach, Joseph (2007). *It*. Ann Arbor: University of Michigan Press.

Robinson, Amy (1996). "Forms of Appearance of Value: Homer Plessy and the Politics of Privacy," in *Performance and Cultural Politics*, ed. Elin Diamond. New York: Routledge, 239–66.

Román, David (1998). *Acts of Intervention: Performance, Gay Culture and AIDS*. Urbana: Indiana University Press.

Salamon, Gayle (2010). *Assuming a Body: Transgender and Rhetorics of Materiality*. New York: Columbia University Press.

Sartre, Jean-Paul (2007). *Existentialism Is a Humanism*. New Haven: Yale University Press.

Schechner, Richard, ed. (2002). "What Is Performance," in *Performance Studies: An Introduction*. London, New York: Routledge, 28–51.

Schleiner, Winfried (2000). "Early Modern Controversies about the One Sex Model," *Renaissance Quarterly* 53.1: 180–91.

Schulman, Sarah (2012). *The Gentrification of the Mind: Book Subtitle: Witness to a Lost Imagination*. Berkeley: University of California Press.

Sharpe, Christina (2016). *In the Wake: On Blackness and Being*. Durham: Duke University Press.

Snorton, C. Riley (2017). *Black on Both Sides: A Racial History of Trans Identity*. Minneapolis: University of Minnesota Press.

Spillers, Hortense (1987). "Mama's Baby, Papa's Maybe: An American Grammar Book," *Diacritics* 17.2: 64–81.

Taylor, Diana (2007). "Translating Performance," in *The Performance Studies Reader*, ed. Henry Bial. London, New York: Routledge, 381–6.

Thompson, Ayanna (2006), "Practicing a Theory/Theorizing a Practice: An Introduction to Shakespearean Colorblind Casting," in *Colorblind Shakespeare: New Perspectives on Race and Performance*, ed. Ayanna Thompson. New York: Routledge, 1–26.

Treneman, Ann (2016). "What a Piece of Art Is This Man: Paapa Essiedu's Painter Hamlet Is a Vivid, Engaging Presence in This New, Africa-Set Production," *The Times,* March 23: 11.

Ward, Candace, ed. (1995). *Everyman and Other Miracle and Morality Plays*. Mineola, NY: Dover Publications.

Wise, Louis (2018). "A Fresh Prince," *Sunday Times*, January: 18.

FURTHER READING

If you would like to explore further, here are some key text to help you make a start.

Audre Lorde's *The Cancer Journals* (San Francisco, CA: Aunt Lute Books, 2006) is a memoir that explores the black feminist writer's experience coping with breast cancer and the impact it had on her personal and political understandings.

Bruce Henderson and Noam Ostrander's *Understanding Disability Studies and Performance Studies* (London and New York: Routledge, 2010) is a collection that brings together disability studies and performance studies, including analysis of photography, film, dance, theater, and performance art.

C. Riley Snorton's *Black on Both Sides: A Racial History of Trans Identity* (Minneapolis: University of Minnesota Press, 2017) offers a genealogy of the relationship between blackness and transness, producing a radical new understanding of gender.

Mel Y. Chen's *Animacies: Biopolitics, Racial Mattering, and Queer Affect* (Durham: Duke University Press, 2012) explores how matter that is considered insensate animates culture.

Nirmala Erevelles' *Disability and Difference in Global Contexts: Enabling a Transformative Body Politic* (New York: Palgrave MacMillan, 2011) offers analysis of disability in a global and economic context. The interdisciplinary study spans the humanities and social sciences.

Simon Shepherd's *Theatre, Body and Pleasure* (London and New York: Routledge, 2006) uses performance theory to explore physicality in theater. The text explores the relationship between time, space, and understandings of the body.

Theri Alyce Pickens' *Black Madness: Mad Blackness* (Durham: Duke University Press, 2019) examines the relationship between blackness and disability using speculative fiction as the case studies in her analysis.

INDEX

Theory for Theatre Studies: Bodies

Online resources to accompany this book are available at https://bloomsbury.pub/theory-for-theatre-studies-bodies. If you experience any problems, please contact Bloomsbury at companionwebsites@bloomsbury.com.

Theory for Theatre Studies meets the need for accessible, mid-length volumes that unpack keywords that lie at the core of the discipline. Aimed primarily at undergraduate students and secondarily at postgraduates and researchers, the volumes feature both background material historicizing the term and original, forward-looking research into intersecting theoretical trends in the field. Case studies ground volumes in praxis, and additional resources online ensure readers are equipped with the necessary skills and understanding as they move deeper into the discipline.

SERIES EDITORS

Susan Bennett, University of Calgary, Canada
Kim Solga, Western University, Canada

Published titles
Theory for Theatre Studies: Space
Kim Solga
Theory for Theatre Studies: Sound
Susan Bennett
Theory for Theatre Studies: Memory
Milija Gluhovic
Theory for Theatre Studies: Emotion
Peta Tait
Theory for Theatre Studies: Movement
Rachel Fensham

Forthcoming titles
Theory for Theatre Studies: Economics
Michael McKinnie
Theory for Theatre Studies: Aesthetics
John Lutterbie